Carmel W

Best Man

B L O O M S B U R Y
LONDON · NEW DELHI · NEW YORK · SYDNEY

Bloomsbury Methuen Drama
An imprint of Bloomsbury Publishing Plc

50 Bedford Square	1385 Broadway
London	New York
WC1B 3DP	NY 10018
UK	USA

www.bloomsbury.com

First published 2013

British Library Cataloguing-in-Publication Data
A catalogue record for this book is available from the British Library.

ISBN: PB: 978-1-4725-3928-1
ePub: 978-1-4725-3930-4
ePdf: 978-1-4725-3929-8

Typeset by Mark Heslington Ltd, Scarborough, North Yorkshire
Printed and bound in Great Britain

The Everyman & Project Arts Centre
in association with Cork Midsummer Festival

BEST MAN

CARMEL WINTERS

Premiered at The Everyman on 21 June 2013 and
performed at The Everyman from 21 to 29 June 2013
as part of Cork Midsummer Festival before transferring
to Project Arts Centre from 17 to 27 July 2013.

Best Man is supported by an Arts Council Theatre Project Award.
The Everyman and Project Arts Centre are both supported by
The Arts Council / An Chomhairle Ealaíon and by Cork City
Council and Dublin City Council respectively.

Cast & Creative Team

Kay	*Derbhle Crotty*
Alan	*Peter Gowen*
Marta	*Kate Stanley Brennan*
Claire	*Róisín O'Neill*
Denis	*Bryan Murray*
Bernadette	*Úna Crawford O'Brien*
Director	*Michael Barker-Caven*
Set and Costume Design	*Liam Doona*
Lighting Design	*Sinéad McKenna*
Music & Sound Design	*Ivan Birthistle and*
	Vincent Doherty
Video Design	*Arnim Friess*
Producers	*Rachel Murray*
	Eimear O'Herlihy
Production Manager	*Lisa Mahony*
Stage Director	*Donna Leonard*
Assistant Stage Managers	*Stephen Manning*
	Josephine Dennehy
Assistant Designer; Costume	*Katie Crowley*
Chief LX	*Kevin Smith (Cork)*
	Eoin McNinch (Dublin)
Set Construction	*Ian Thompson*
Scenic Art	*Vincent Bell*

The production team would like to thank the following: Sylvia Meulmeester and Hotel Isaacs Cork, Kearney+Melia Communications, Kate Bowe PR, The Shelbourne Bar Cork, Jesamine Humphreys, Eimer and David at The Abbey Theatre, Val and Jim at The Gate Theatre, Mick and Colm at the Samuel Beckett Theatre, Barry Conway at The Lir, Linda and all at Leinster Cricket Club, JS Dobbs & Co Ltd, Healthcare Supplies Dublin.

Best Man was originally commissioned by Abbey Theatre Amharclann na Mainistreach.

This production has been licensed by arrangement with The Agency (London) Ltd, 24 Pottery Lane, London W11 4LZ, info@theagency.co.uk

Please note the text of the play which appears in this volume may be changed during the rehearsal process and appear in a slightly altered form in performance.

BEST MAN
CARMEL WINTERS

CARMEL WINTERS
WRITER

Carmel studied Drama and English at Trinity College Dublin where she was awarded several prizes for outstanding academic achievement. Her debut art-house feature film *Snap*, received its World Premiere at the Tribeca Film Festival in New York in April 2010 and was awarded Best Irish Film and Best Irish Director by the Dublin Film Critics' Circle at the Jameson Dublin International Film Festival 2011. It was selected as Variety Critics' Choice Award at Karlovy-Vary International Film Festival and was voted Best Film at the Cinemateca International Film Festival in Uruguay.

Her most recent theatre play *B for Baby* (produced by the Abbey Theatre), won the Irish Times Irish Theatre Award for Best New Play in 2010. She recently completed residencies at the National Theatre, London, and Centre Culturel Irlandais, Paris, and is currently preparing to direct her next feature film and working on a new commission for the Abbey Theatre, Dublin. Carmel is currently Theatre Artist in Residence at the Everyman.

Carmel has also lectured in Drama at both Trinity College Dublin and, most recently, in the University of East Anglia where she taught Creative Writing (Drama).

THE EVERYMAN

The Everyman, as the primary venue in Cork for middle-scale local, national and international productions, presents work by companies such as Druid, Red Kettle, London Classic Theatre, Corn Exchange, Landmark Productions, Ouroboros as well as providing an important platform for local and emerging theatrical talent. The Everyman and Cork Operatic Society's co-production of Pagliacci was awarded Best Opera of 2012 in the Irish Times Theatre Awards.

BOARD: Michael White (*Chairman*), Cllr. Tim Brosnan, Ted Mahon Buckley, Brendan Casserly, Cllr. Lorraine Kingston, Dick Langford, Dick Lehane, Denis McSweeney, Leachlainn O'Cathain and Michael Twomey.

Eimear O'Herlihy (*Executive Director*), Michael Barker-Caven (*Artistic Director*), Kaye Keating (*Finance Manager*), Robbie Cotter (*Box Office & Building Manager*), Naomi Daly (*Production Assistant*), Melanie Kavanagh (*Marketing Manager*), Ana Feria (*Marketing Manager – Acting*), Mark Donovan (*Technical Manager*), Brian Mitchell (*Assistant Technical Manager*), Nathan Cassidy (*Bar Manager*), Kearney+Melia Communications (*PR*). Thank you to all our FOH Voluntary Staff.

The Everyman, 15 MacCurtain Street, Cork, Ireland
www.everymancork.com

PROJECT ARTS CENTRE

Project Arts Centre is Ireland's leading centre for the presentation and development of contemporary art, dedicated to protecting the independent sector and nurturing the next generation of Irish artists across all forms of the performing and visual arts.

BOARD: John Collins (*Chairman*), Louise Church, Loughlin Deegan, Sarah Glennie, Dylan Haskins, Phillip McMahon, Sarah Pierce.

Cian O'Brien (*Artistic Director*), Niamh O'Donnell (*General Manager & Executive Producer*), Tessa Giblin (*Curator of Visual Arts*), Ciara McKeon (*Assistant Curator of Visual Arts*), Annette Devoy (*Administrator*), Kate McSweeney (*Finance & Accounts Manager*), Joseph 'JC' Collins (*Production Manager*), Seán Dennehy (*Technical Manager*), Carmel Mackey (*House Manager*), Melanie Wright (*Communications Manager*), Kate Heffernan (*Assistant Producer*), Kate O'Sullivan (*Development & Communications Officer*), Andrew Adamson (*Bar Manager*).

Project Arts Centre, 39 East Essex Street, Temple Bar, Dublin 2, Ireland *www.projectartscentre.ie*

Cast & Creative Team

DERBHLE CROTTY
Kay

Derbhle's theatre work includes *The Dead* (Abbey and Peacock Theatre), *Dubliners* (Gaiety Theatre), *Crave/ Illusions* (Actor's Touring Company), *The Beauty Queen of Leenane* (Young Vic), *The Field* (The Olympia Theatre), *The Silver Tassie, The Gigli Concert, Sive, The Good Father, Gaslight* and *The Playboy of the Western World* (Druid), *Dubliners, Cat on a Hot Tin Roof* and *Everyday* (Corn Exchange), *Marble, An Ideal Husband, The Three Sisters, A Month in the Country, The Dandy Dolls, Beauty in a Broken Place, The Plough and the Stars, Bailegangaire, Portia Coughlan, The Mai, Katie Roche* and *The Well of the Saints* (Abbey Theatre), *The Home Place, Dancing at Lughnasa* (Gate Theatre), *I'll Be The Devil, Little Eyolf, Camino Real, Hamlet* and *Macbeth, Macbett, Penelopiad* (Royal Shakespeare Company), *The Alice Trilogy, The Weir, The Playboy of the Western World, Summerfolk* and *The Merchant of Venice* (Royal Court Theatre), *Playing the Wife* (Chichester Festival Theatre) and *Royal Supreme* (Theatre Royal, Plymouth).

Film and television work includes *Noble* (Stephen Bradley, Destiny Films), *The Clinic, Gold in the Streets* (RTÉ), *Any Time Now* (Nora Films Ltd), *Poorhouse* (Ocean Film Productions), *Stella Days* (Newgrange Pictures), *Notes on a Scandal* (Scott Rudin Productions) and *Inside I'm Dancing* (Momentum Pictures). Radio work includes *Myrrha, The Weight of Water* and *St Patrick's Daughter* (BBC), *Broken Moon, The Gospels of Aughamore, Portia Coughlan, Bailegangaire, King Lear* and *Quinn* (RTÉ)

PETER GOWEN
Alan

Peter most recently wrote and appeared in his new one-man show *The Chronicles of Oggle* directed by Donal Gallagher for Asylum Theatre Company at the Everyman and in venues throughout

Cork. Peter's appearances at Abbey Theatre, Dublin include *Observe the Sons of Ulster Marching Towards The Somme*, *A Whistle in the Dark*, *A Child's Christmas in Wales*, *Madigan's Lock*, *Shadow of a Gunman* and in Aidan Matthews' *Communion*. Peter appeared at the Gate Theatre, Dublin as Michael in Joe Dowling's recent production of Brian Friel's *Dancing at Lughnasa*. He appeared as Christy in the West End production of Martin McDonagh's *The Lieutenant of Inishmore* at the Garrick. Other theatre credits include *Shadow of a Gunman*, *Death of a Salesman*, *Philadelphia Here I Come!*, *Translations*, *Fathers and Sons*, *A Touch of the Poet*, *The Country Boy*, *The Beauty Queen of Leenane*, and West End productions of *The Plough and The Stars* and *A Doll's House*. He also appeared in Mark Doherty's *Trad*, winner of Fringe First Award at the Edinburgh Festival 2005. Peter appeared in *Anna Karenina* directed by Michael Barker-Caven at the Gate Theatre, Dublin and as Reverend Hale in *The Crucible* directed by Patrick Mason at the Abbey Theatre, Dublin. He appeared in *The Final Shot* directed by Tim Roseman at Theatre503 in London and in the leading role of Yank in *The Hairy Ape* by Eugene O'Neill directed by Pat Kiernan for Corcadorca Theatre Company. Television and film credits include *Love/Hate*, *The Tudors*, *My Boy Jack*, *The Bill*, *Paradise Club*, *Minder*, *Coronation Street*, *On Home Ground*, *Who Bombed Birmingham?*, *Eat the Peach*, *The Butcher Boy*, *Dancing at Lughnasa*, *A Love Divided* and *Breakfast On Pluto*

KATE STANLEY BRENNAN
Marta

Kate's theatre credits include *The Plough and the Stars* (Abbey Theatre/tour), *Tiny Plays for Ireland* (Fishamble), *The Making of 'Tis Pity She's a Whore* (Siren), *Foxfinder* (Theatre503), *Feel Sad About Japan* (Southwark Playhouse/Nabakov), *Yerma* (West Yorkshire Playhouse), *The Sanctuary Lamp* (Arcola Theatre, London), *Terminus* (tour), *The Playboy of the Western World*, *The Resistible Rise of Arturo Ui* and *Saved* (Abbey Theatre), *Love and Money* (Hatch, Best Actress Nomination), *Last Days of Judas Iscariot* (Making Strange, Best Supporting Actress Nomination), *Caligula* (CHRG/Dublin Theatre Festival), *Translations* (Ouroboros), *Salomé* (Gate Theatre), *Mother*

Goose (Gaiety Theatre), *Macbeth* (Second Age) and *Sonnets for an Old Century* (X-Belair). Film and television credits include *Dollhouse* (Best Acting Award Odessa Film Festival: dir. Kirsten Sheridan), *Chasing Leprechauns* (Hallmark), *Thanks for Nothing* (Redomlette), *Dublin in Pieces* (i-wire films), *Speed Dating* (System Forty Eight) and *The Tudors* (Showtime), Isabella in *Fair City* and *RAW* (RTÉ). Kate has performed in several plays for radio including the award-winning *Twenty-Seven* (RTÉ).

RÓISÍN O'NEILL
Claire

Róisín was born to Irish parents in Canberra, Australia, but moved to Cork at the age of four. Throughout her youth she attended part-time classes at CADA performing arts and limelight stage school where she insisted she was studying 'screech and drama'. Once she left school Róisín went on to study Drama and Theatre Studies in UCC. While at UCC she was an active member of the Dramat Society. During her first year in college she played the Princess in *Aladdin*, the Everyman Pantomime. In 2011 she played Cassie in *Latch* (Hammergrin), a piece of new writing and a site-specific piece which was part of Cork Midsummer Festival. Over the past two years she has also begun film acting. This year she appeared as Emma Walsh in TV3's *Deception* and will also appear in Brendan Muldowney's new film *Love Eternal* which is due to be released later in 2013.

BRYAN MURRAY
Denis

Bryan's theatre work includes *The Hostage, Borstal Boy, The Morning After Optimism, The Shadow of a Gunman, The Silver Tassie, Deathwatch, The Devils, Saint Joan, Blood Wedding, Philadelphia Here I Come!, The Rivals, Volunteers, The Glass Menagerie, The Shadow of the Glen, The Whiteheaded Boy, Fando and Lis, The Plebeians Rehearse the Uprising, The Happy Go Likeable Man, A Change of Mind, The Plough and the*

Stars, Juno and the Paycock, Catchpenny Twist, Nashville New York, Blood Brothers, The Miss Firecracker Contest, Finian's Rainbow, One Touch of Venus, Misery, Deathtrap, The Cavalcaders, Boyband, An Inspector Calls, An Ideal Husband, Joe and I, The Goat, Love Letters, Rank, Medea, Anna Karenina, Salomé, Great Expectations, The Deep Blue Sea, Celebration, My Cousin Rachel.

He has been a regular face on television for the last 35 years, probably best known for his roles as Fitz in *Strumpet City*, Flurry Knox in *The Irish RM*, Shifty in *Bread* (for which he won BBC TV Personality Of The Year), Harry Cassidy in *Perfect Scoundrels*, Trevor Jordache in *Brookside* and Bob Charles in *Fair City*. His other television work includes *The Year of the French, I'm a Dreamer Montreal, Rifleman, Bread or Blood, Final Run, Iris in the Traffic, The Franchise Affair, Gates of Gold, Hard Shoulder, The Trials of Oscar Wilde, Casualty, Holby City, The Bill, Silent Witness* and *Proof*.

He presented the children's series *Knock Knock* and *Umbrella* for BBC Television for three years, *Encore* and *Saturday Night Live* for RTÉ. He recently presented the IFTA nominated documentary series *The Tenements,* and the four-part documentary series *The Big House* for TV3. He occasionally presents *Late Date* on RTÉ Radio 1.

ÚNA CRAWFORD O'BRIEN
Bernadette

Úna wanted to be an actress from the time she won her first medal in the Father Mathew Feis at the age of four. Her first professional production was in *Death and the Maiden* in Andrews Lane Theatre when she played the part of Paulina. This was followed by *Collected Stories* at the Civic Theatre, *Deadline, Out of Order Sweetie,* and *4 Play* at Andrews Lane and *How the Other Half Loves* in Andrews Lane and the Tivoli. She twice toured the country with *Love Letters* and played to packed houses in *Grumpy Old Women* in the Gaiety Theatre and theatres across the country. *Menopause the Musical* in the Tivoli was an equal success.

Her film and television work includes *Three Wise Women* (Hallmark), *Love on the Line* (Irish Dream Films), *A Very Unlucky Leprechaun*

(Concorde) and *Single Handed* (RTÉ). She has done various readings for *The View* (RTÉ). Úna has played Renee Phelan in *Fair City* since 1998.

MICHAEL BARKER-CAVEN
Director

Michael is Artistic Director of the Everyman. For Ouroboros (previously Theatreworks), for whom Michael was Artistic Director between 1995 and 2004, credits include *Amadeus* by Peter Shaffer, *Richard II, Macbeth, Richard III* (nominated Best Director 2001 Irish Theatre Awards), *Troilus and Cressida* and *Venus and Adonis,* all by William Shakespeare, *Tales From Ovid* by Ted Hughes (nominated Special Judges Award 2002 Irish Theatre Awards), the Irish Premiere of *Mutabilitie* by Frank McGuinness, *Anna Karenina* by Helen Edmundson (nominated Best Director 1998 Irish Theatre Awards) and *The Fetishist* by Michel Tournier. For Landmark Productions, the acclaimed Irish premieres of *Skylight* by David Hare, *The Goat, or Who is Sylvia?* by Edward Albee, *Blackbird* by David Harrower and *Miss Julie* in a version by Frank McGuinness, all at the Project Arts Centre; *Alice in Wonderland*, in a version by Mary Elizabeth Burke-Kennedy and *The Secret Garden*, adapted by Neil Duffield, both co-productions with the Helix, and the premieres of *Dandelions* and *October* by Fiona Looney, both in co-production with MCD Productions at the Olympia Theatre. In London's West End, the 2007/8 award-winning revival of *Shadowlands* by Bill Nicholson which opened at the Wyndham's Theatre, before transferring for a further successful run at the Novello Theatre. At the Gate Theatre, where Michael was previously Head of Creative Development, acclaimed productions of *Little Women* by Louisa May Alcott (in a version by Anne-Marie Casey), *Les Liaisons Dangereuses* by Christopher Hampton, *Anna Karenina* by Helen Edmundson, *Old Times* by Harold Pinter (as part of the playwright's 75th birthday celebrations), *Play* for the 2006 Centenary Celebration of the work of Samuel Beckett at the Gate and the Barbican, London, *The Shape of Things* by Neil LaBute (nominated Best Director 2002 Irish Theatre Awards), and *Therese Raquin* by Emile Zola (in a version by Nicholas Wright). Opera credits include co-direction on *Pagliacci* by Leoncavallo, for the Everyman/Cork Operatic Society, as part of the 2012 Cork Midsummer Festival (Winner, Best Opera Production, 2012 Irish Theatre Awards); *Medea* for Glimmerglass Opera, New York, *The Duenna* by Richard Brinsley Sheridan, ETO/Royal Opera House and on tour in the UK, *Transformations* by Conrad Susa/Anne Sexton (Winner, Best Opera Production, 2006 Irish Theatre Awards) and *The Mines of Sulphur* by Richard Rodney Bennett, (Winner, Best Opera Production, 2008 Irish Theatre Awards) for Wexford Festival Opera.

LIAM DOONA
Set and Costume Design

Liam is a freelance theatre designer and Head of the Department of Design and Visual Arts at Dun Laoghaire Institute of Art, Design and Technology. Alongside his educational work he has maintained a busy practice as set and costume designer. Notable productions include *The Death of Harry Leon* (Ouroboros), *To Kill a Mockingbird* (York Theatre Royal and national tour), *The White Album* (Nottingham Playhouse), *Romeo and Juliet* (York Theatre Royal), *Boys Stuff* (Sheffield Crucible), *The Rivals, Endgame, The Merchant of Venice* and *The Seagull* (national British tours with Compass Theatre).

Liam's work was included in the *Collaborators* exhibition at the Victoria and Albert Museum, London. He writes for The Blue Pages – The Journal of the Society of British Theatre Designers, and his work can be seen in '2D 3D' (2002) and 'Collaborators' (2007), the quadrennial reviews of British Stage Design published by SBTD. His study of American designer Jo Mielziner was recently republished in *A Reader in Scenography*, (Routledge).

SINÉAD McKENNA
Lighting Design

Sinéad's designs include *Howie The Rookie, Greener, October, The Last Days of The Celtic Tiger* and *Blackbird* (Landmark), *Pageant* and *Swept*

(CoisCéim), *Zoe's Play* (The Ark), *Quietly, Alice in Funderland, The Plough and the Stars, 16 Possible Glimpses, The Burial at Thebes, Howie The Rookie* and *Finders Keepers* (Abbey/Peacock), *Dubliners*, (Corn Exchange/Dublin Theatre Festival), *Travesties, The Importance of Being Earnest, Improbable Frequency* (New York Drama Desk nomination 2009), *The Parker Project, Life is a Dream, Attempts on her Life* and *Dream of Autumn* (Rough Magic), *New Electric Ballroom* (Druid), *The Making of 'Tis Pity She's a Whore, The Lulu House* and *Medea* (Siren Productions), *Philadelphia Here I Come!* (Longroad), *Private Lives* (The Gate), *A Skull in Connemara, Faith Healer* and *Doubt* (Decadent/Town Hall Productions), *Dancing At Lughnasa, Hamlet, A Doll's House, Macbeth, Philadelphia Here I Come!, Othello* and *How Many Miles to Babylon* (Second Age), *Pineapple, All About Town* and *Wunderkind* (Calipo), *Macbeth, The Snow Queen* and *Merry Christmas Betty Ford* (Lyric Theatre). She designed *Ladies and Gents* –Best Lighting Design Irish Theatre Awards (Semper Fi).

Recent opera designs include *Opera Briefs* (The Lir), *The Magic Flute, The Marriage of Figaro* (Opera Theatre Company), *Midsummer Night's Dream* (Opera Ireland) and *La Traviata* (Malmo Opera House). Designs for comedy include Des Bishop, Tommy Tiernan, Neil Delamere and Maeve Higgins.

IVAN BIRTHISTLE AND VINCENT DOHERTY
Music & Sound Design

Ivan and Vincent work together on an ongoing collaborative basis. Past work includes *Missing, Pageant, Touch Me, Swimming With My Mother, As You Are/Faun, Boxes* (CoisCéim), *Romeo And Juliet* (Second Age), *Re-energize, Over The Wire* (Derry Playhouse), *The Picture Of Dorian Gray, It Only Ever Happens In The Movies, No Escape, Playboy of the Western World, Saved, The Alice Trilogy* and *True West* (The Abbey), *The Great Goat Bubble, Tiny Plays For Ireland 1+2, End Of The Road, Big Ol' Piece of Cake, Rank, Noah and the Tower Flower, The Gist of It, Monged* and *Tadgh Stray Wandered In* (Fishamble), *Dockers, The Absence of Women, The Beauty Queen of Leenane, Homeplace, Dancing at Lughnasa, Much Ado About Nothing, Shadow of a Gunman* and *True*

West (The Lyric), *The Field* (Lane Productions), *The Boys of Foley Street*, *Laundry* (ANU Productions), *Freefall, Mud, Foley* and *Lolita* (Corn Exchange), *All in the Timing* (Innis Theatre Co.), *The Sanctuary Lamp* and *Honour* (B'spoke), *Dying City, Pentecost* (Rough Magic), *This Is Our Youth, Wedding Day at the Cro-Magnons', Roberto Zucco, This is Not a Life, Beckett's Ghosts, Shooting Gallery, Far Away* and *The Massacre @ Paris* (Bedrock), *Miss Julie* and *Blackbird* (Landmark), *Ladies and Gents, God's Grace, Adrenalin* and *Slaughter* (Semper Fi).

ARNIM FRIESS
Video Design

Arnim specialises in designing dynamic performance environments, blending lighting, video, photography and motion graphics. His lighting and projection designs have been seen not only in theatres around the world, but also in a zoo, a monastery, an abandoned pub and deep down in a cave. Recent designs include *Ghosts in the Wall* for the RSC, *42nd Street* and *Gypsy* at the Curve, Leicester, *Ravenboy* at Jacksons Lane, *Fog* at the Finborough Theatre, *Wander* at the Jockey Club Theatre, Hong Kong, the National Holocaust Memorial Day, *The Rememberers* for Birmingham Rep, a roof of light for Coventry Cathedral's Blitz commemoration, *Lucky Seven* for Hampstead Theatre, *Looking for JJ* for Pilot Theatre at the Unicorn, *One Night in November* for the Belgrade Theatre, Coventry, *The Suicide* and *An Inspector Calls* at Theatr Clwyd, *The White Album* at the Nottingham Playhouse. *www.pixelbox.ltd.uk*

KATIE CROWLEY
Assistant Designer; Costume

Katie is a graduate of Design for Stage and Screen: Costume, at Dun Laoghaire Institute of Art, Design and Technology.

Best Man

Characters

Kay, *early 40s*
Alan, *the same or slightly younger*
Marta, *their children's nanny, 30*
Claire, *Kay and Alan's daughter, 17*
Denis, *Marta's father, 80*
Bernadette, *Denis's home-help, 50*

Setting: to represent variously the home of Denis, a retired Ambassador; Kay and Alan's house; the 'flat'

Time: now (final scene), and six years prior

Scene One

Alan and Kay's bedroom. Alan is in bed jotting notes and arranging papers into various bundles on the quilt. Kay comes in, whiskey in one hand, remote in the other. She switches on the television, finds Top Gear.

She sips her whiskey and undresses while keeping a keen eye on the screen, at last attempting to climb into her side of the bed.

Alan   Two ticks, nearly finished. Did you say goodnight?

Beat.

Claire made me promise you'd tuck them in. Said she'd know if you hadn't if they woke up without lipstick on their cheeks.

Kay   Should I get Myles up to make another pee?

Alan   No, I've done it. Just leave them their kiss.

Kay *tops up her lipstick and exits, returning moments later as* **Alan** *adds the final document to his constellation of papers.*

Alan   There. Your husband has divined the game plan behind human relationships – it's as perfectly constelled as a solar system . . .

Kay   You might shuffle 'the solar system' over to your side of the bed so I can get in.

Alan   The small change of where you live, with who, how long – that's just surface décor, a little local colour – when you strip it all away every couple collapses into one of these.

Kay   An A-4 sheet to fit every bed?

Alan   A meets B and (*Snaps his fingers.*) the whole shebang is set up and strait-jacketed, everything that's ever happened and everything that can ever happen between you signed, sealed and delivered. Once you unravel a couple's first encounter, you can just roll out the rest.

Kay *ups the volume on Top Gear.*

Alan   It's not the first impression. It's the first deal, the first *transaction* that's replayed over and over again. Take you and me that first Monday of Fresher's Week. I'm flogging the intellectual cachet of the Philosophical Society, you're showing remarkable enthusiasm for the free whiskey . . .

Kay   That wasn't our first 'transaction'.

Alan   Yes it was, I distinctly remember – in the time it took to interest you in our inaugural debate you had emptied six tumblers.

Kay   They weren't tumblers, they were thimbles. And that was our second transaction, the first was at the Open Day six months previous. You had a screaming baby strapped to your back and were demanding to know if the University provided creche facilities.

Alan   Had I?

Kay   The girls were all fawning over the 'new man'. It was very canny of you, hijacking your niece to launch your academic career.

Alan (*remembering*)   It must have been when my sister had her appendix out . . . The poor child was inconsolable – not for her mother as everyone assumed – simply because she was cutting back teeth. I have no recollection of you being there . . .

Kay   Why would you? I wasn't the one backpacking a bawling infant.

Alan   It doesn't count if I wasn't aware of you. It has to be two-way, otherwise it's not a transaction. Our defining encounter was, like I said, me trying to engage you in a meaningful discussion about life while you slugged back the Powers. And here we are, twenty years later . . .

Kay   It's Green Spot, not Powers.

Alan   Same poison, different brand. Imagining we're authors of our relationships is laughable. We're little better

than rats – deranged rodents scurrying down the same
cheesy rat runs over and over again. That's why the wedding
speech is so crucial.

Kay (*doubtful*)   It is . . .

Alan   The best man's job is to gas-light the guests with
entertaining yarns of Bob and Ann's one-in-a-million match.
He's the one charged with painting a picture of the grand
adventure ahead as the groom tackles new frontiers with
his one-and-only. In other words the best man's got to come
up with the cover-up story. And you know why they come
to me?

Kay   Because you're an incurable romantic and you charge
per word, not per speech.

Alan   After months of scribbling on matchboxes and beer-
mats all they can manage to come up with is one cliché, one
paralysing platitude after another. They think it's them,
'they can't write' – in truth it's this . . . (*The papers spread on the
bed.*) This frozen constellation makes a pair of automated
monkeys out of every married couple.

Kay   That's not going into your next speech, I hope.

Alan   I'm saving it for the novel.

Kay   Ah.

Alan   What – 'Ah'.

Kay   Nothing. Only I thought you had three 'cover-ups' to
be written by this weekend.

Alan   I do. That's why I've had to rationalise the whole
operation. What I've done is, I've amalgamated all the
speeches I've written so far and come up with a series of
seven Masters. So next time a sweaty little groomsman logs
onto oscarweddingspeeches-dot-com I merely have to match
the couple to the prototype and – ching – press PayPal, do
pass 'go', do collect five hundred pounds.

Kay   If one in seven couples gets the exact same speech, what's to stop them downloading one from the internet?

Alan   Not the 'exact same' obviously. I insert a few identifying details here and there, drop in an anecdote or two . . . Point is, I don't have to build the entire speech from scratch every time. This way, I know where the front door is, the back door, how to get in and out of the building . . .

Kay   God, Jeremy, I could do better on a push bike!

He grabs the remote control, turns off Top Gear, then huffily packs away his prototypes.

Kay   Alan, please, no tantrums. I've been traipsing your automated monkeys around a maze of houses all day – my brain needs flatline entertainment, not mental gymnastics.

Alan   I have to listen to you and your grimy dollar and dime deals day-in day-out.

Kay   My grimy deals put this roof over our heads in case you've forgotten.

Alan   Fine. I'll shut up. Raising our children by day and earning 'pin money' by night clearly doesn't entitle a man to airtime in his own home.

Kay   You're putting words in my mouth.

Alan   Yes, that's precisely what I do, put *my* words in other people's lazy mouths. I didn't give up a respectable career in medicine to ventriloquise best man speeches!

You need to get yourself another skivvy. I can't even begin to contemplate any kind of serious work in this set up! What am I supposed to do – dash off chapters in between dropping Claire to tennis and collecting Myles from school? The speeches were meant to be a stop-gap, something to keep me limbered up, not the be-all and end-all! The frustrating thing is that the novel's practically written – I can hear the damn thing spooling in my head – finding the time to write it down is the problem.

Kay   You have mornings when the children are at school. And nights, I am home most nights.

Alan   That's alright for this monkey-business, the novel needs better conditions.

Kay   Like?

Beat.

Alan   The novel needs a nanny.

She erupts in laughter.

Kay   Oh, Alan . . . You refused a nanny for the children. Now you want a nanny for your novel?

Alan   I'll pay for her. If this system works out, I can up output to seven or eight speeches a month – that should cover her wages.

Kay   Don't be ridiculous. If you're writing more wedding speeches to pay a nanny's wages where are you going to find the time to write your novel? It's precisely that kind of dead-end logic keeps the rats on the rat-run long after the cheese has been scoffed.

Beat.

I'll pay if you're actually serious about this . . .

Alan   You could write her off as a business expense – list her as an associate agent or something.

Kay   How do you know it'll be a 'her'? I might fancy a handsome young Puerto-Rican with corkscrew curls and a pert bum. Or a French man like the one in the Kerrygold ad – 'Is zere somezing I can 'elp?'

Alan   'Well, you can put a bit of butter on the spuds, Andre . . .'

Kay   I loved that ad.

Alan   Course you did. That's why it won't be a 'he'.

Kay   You trust you more than you trust me?

Alan   Absolutely.

Kay   I'll email a few agencies tomorrow. See who's available – at what price.

Scene Two

Alan *and* **Kay**'s *kitchen. An overlapping conversation as* **Kay** *is on the phone and* **Alan** (*off*) *is ushering someone to the door.*

Alan   Bye, bye-bye, don't forget – right at the end of the road. Left-hand side for the centre. Every twenty minutes or so – except of course on Sundays.

Kay (*on the phone*)   Absolutely! No reason we can't nail this thing!

Alan   It's exact fare only so if you need some change . . . ? Right. Bye now.

Kay   I'm not convinced that's the best card to play here . . .

Alan   No, thank *you*, thank you very much, we'll be in touch.

Kay   Tomorrow at four. Lovely.

Hangs up.

Alan   Take care . . . Bye, bye-bye, bye . . .

Alan *joins* **Kay** *in the kitchen. He shuts the window, warms his hands at the Aga.*

Alan   God that was grim. Like a particularly bad parade of Rose of Tralee contestants. I'm beginning to think we should hire the first girl to admit she despises children but she does need a roof over her head – and a small stipend to support her dope habit. (*The phone.*) Who was that?

Kay   Harrington, your ex-boss. He wants me to give a 'conservative' i.e. low evaluation on the Mespil Road property, his soon-to-be ex-wife is taking him to the cleaners.

Alan   He didn't ask about me?

Kay   He said to tell you the Nigerian that replaced you is nearing the end of his contract if you have had, I quote, 'enough gap years to satisfy your delayed adolescence'.

Alan   The cheek of him! What did you say?

Kay   I said if I quoted too low his wife's solicitor would authorise their own evaluation – and go through every other estimate with a fine tooth comb.

Alan   'Delayed adolescence', how dare he! I've a good mind to call his wife and tell her about the shenanigans with the Bosnian intern! The girl still had braces, for God's sake! That's how we spotted what was going on – the state of his lips. Like they'd been through a cheese grater!

Kay   Right. The Super Nanny Contest. Top three.

Alan   You can go first.

Kay   No, you; I want to know what you want in my substitute. The woman I'll be paying to cover my defecit.

Alan   Besides a little air space and large breasts?

Kay   You've led me to believe your mother put you off large breasts.

Alan   Being breast-fed in the back of a Land Rover outside the school gates does leave a certain aftertaste, it's true . . .

Kay   Eugh, when I hear of mothers like that I'm almost glad I never had one . . .

Alan   I doubt yours would have been the clay hut type – not if you're anything to go by . . . Imagine having to face into thirty mocking children in the classroom after that, the woman should have been jailed for child abuse!

Kay   The Bolivian Rose was interesting . . .

Alan   Marta Morales. Yes, I thought so too . . . (*Consulting the notes.*) 'Studying for a post-graduate diploma in child psychology'. That ticks the IQ requirement box . . . And I quite fancy reviving my Spanglish. 'Te presento a Marta, nuestra niñera. Está estudiando psicología . . .'

Kay   It's hardly necessary, her English is better than yours.

Alan   Excellent, she can write my novel *and* take care of my kids. 'Gap years!' I'd like to see Harrington attempt to raise two children. He doesn't even know what age his are. I asked him one day and the matron had to correct him!

Kay   There's something daunting about her. The kitchen seemed, I don't know, smaller with her in it. As if she were the one vetting us, not the other way round.

Alan   Latin Americans are like that. Comfortable in their skin, brazenly at home in their bodies. Compared to them we're like awkward visitors tip-toeing around our own anatomies trying to not break anything!

She raises an eyebrow at that.

Alan   The children will like her well enough. She won't have any trouble asserting herself.

Kay   I'm not sure I like the idea of a budding psychologist watching my every move.

Alan   Yes, well, looking at the barrel-scraping alternatives, I say we should seize the opportunity. Why not? Miss Morales can go right ahead – flush out our failings, nip our children's complexes while they're in the bud – before they grow up and turn our grandchildren against us.

Kay   Flush out my failings, you mean. She was practically swooning with admiration for you. The stay-at-home Super-Dad . . . It was the same growing up – all the women in our townland practically falling over each other to rescue my poor widowed father, scrambling to save him from a job every mother is expected to do with her eyes shut and her hands tied!

Alan I can't say I noticed a bias.

Kay No one does when it's in their favour.

A sudden thud against the window. He looks out.

Alan It's our little red robin not quite bob bob bobbin' . . .
He must have assumed the window was open.

Alan *goes out the backdoor, returns with the robin on his palm.*

Alan I'll wait until the kids come home to bury him. They
demand funerary rites for every dead bee and bird these
days. They seem to think mortality's a feast of fizzy drinks
and contraband crisps.

Pause. **Kay** *strokes the dead robin's feathers.*

Kay She's not beautiful, is she?

Alan Who's not?

Kay The nanny. Marta.

Alan Not classically beautiful, no.

Kay But she has a 'someone' in the vicinity, a 'someone'
who brought her here . . .?

Alan 'Had'. It's over now.

Beat.

Kay When did she tell you that?

Alan She didn't. She used the word 'had', not 'has' –
past tense.

Scene Three

*The large reception through to hallway of a Georgian house, its
period features intact beneath years of neglect and declining
batchelorhood.*

*Everywhere there are random piles of memorabilia and debris. An
attempt at order and inventory is evident through the peeling yellow
Post-its dotted about the room.*

a blaring alarm throughout the house. We hear
ᴖ another part of the house as someone tries
. oell rings again. A woman on the brink of
◟ from the exterior façade, checks, then rings again.
.arta.

ɪnside a man whose grandeur is as ruined as the house he lives in makes painful progress with the help of a walking stick (or two) and the hindrance of partially undone trousers.

He picks up the telephone.

Denis Yes?

Beat. He replaces the telephone, ponders. The door bell rings again. He realises his mistake.

Come in! It's open.

The door is a long way off; his hip is locked.

I said come in, you fool, it's on the latch!

Marta *enters.*

Denis Are you deaf? Didn't you hear me calling?

Added to the early signs of dementia is some deafness, as we shall see.

The kitchen's that way. The disherwasher doesn't work and the washing machine leaks. You can organise to get it fixed or not, that's up to you. The last one rinsed things by hand – or dipped them in and out of a bucket, more like – I'm wearing the stains since. You speak English, I presume?

Marta Yes. I speak English.

Denis Not that it's an advantage . . . She's gone back now. To Brazil. Her eldest was turning delinquent – the old grandmother couldn't cope, went on strike, started refusing the monthly cheques. Shut the door. Three days it takes this graveyard to heat up, five minutes and it's an ice box again. You can leave the milk out and it'll keep for a week. Italian?

Marta *stares at him.*

Denis   Portuguese? The latest one they sent me was from
Bray. I sent her back on the same bus that dropped her – the
Irish don't know how to serve, never did. 'Cultural memory'
according to the Aussie Ambass; I call it congenital laziness
coupled with persistent, malicious delusions of upperosity.
The barmbrack's the proof of it, who else would think of
stuffing a confectionery full of secret weaponry? I almost
choked on the coin when I was four, lacerated my throat on
a splintered matchstick when I was five – you know what that
means? It means the Bridgets were out to get me even then!
Help me get this thing up – I can't hold onto my cage and
hoist at the same time.

He claws his trousers. She doesn't budge to help.

Denis   What's wrong with you? Haven't you seen an old
arse before? Be grateful you don't have to wipe it. It's on the
roster, you know, Thursday morning – assisted bath. Then
it's the bi-weekly outing to the dialysis clinic. You drive? It's
hard to find a homehelp who does – you know how much
they charge for taxis in this country? I could travel the
length and breadth of India in a rickshaw for a roundtrip to
the supermarket!

Marta   I'm not your home help.

Denis   What? They don't send good-looking ones to read
the meter . . .

Marta   I haven't come to wash your vests or read your
meter. I'm Marta. Your daughter.

Beat.

Denis   My . . .

Marta (*loud*)   Your daughter!

Denis   I heard you, don't raise your voice at me!

Several beats.

Denis   'Marta' . . . From Bolivia? No . . .

Marta   How many of us are there? One for every post?

Denis   There's James, the eldest, his brood . . .

He indicates the rubble of photos and letters on the mantelpiece.

The wife keeps in touch, sends me regular bulletins –
birthdays, first tooth, last curl, who's the spit of who.
Keeping her foot in the door, I suppose, her hand in the old
pocket. 'Marta . . .'

He fumbles for a yellow Post-it pad and pen.

Short-term's on the blink like everything else around
here – hence the what's-its . . . 'M-A-R-T-A . . .'

*He writes her name in block capitals on the Post-it, underlines it and
sticks it to the mirror above the mantelpiece.*

*When he turns back he sees her examining the framed pictures on the
wall above a deep dresser.*

Found yourself?

Marta   No.

Denis   That's not you? There, the one with the silver
what's-it . . . ? It must be one of James's then . . . I can't get
close enough to see . . . I've instructed the help to move it
but drilling a hole is yet another item they can't seem to
locate on the job description. So, mind you, is insolence and
impertinence – they don't seem to have any difficulty
offering that little extra gratis!

Marta *is about to go.*

Denis   November fourth. Is that your birthday?

She turns back again.

Denis   You're Guadalupe's girl . . .

He peers at her through his magnifying glass.

You don't look like her. Lupita had magnificent hair. Like a
rope through your fist, the weight of it, a fisherman's rope.
She only ever let it down to dry. She'd lie face down on the

flags with it spread out before her steaming in the sun . . .
Still has it, I hope, she hasn't cut it?

Marta   I look like you.

Denis   You do? Your mother tell you that? I was handsome
once, women liked the look of me. Six four I measured in
my socks, now my hat barely touches the six foot peg in the
doctor's surgery. That's five inches I've lost up the way,
another eight about the chest. Even my feet have dropped
two sizes! Where do they go – the kilos, the inches – does hell
have a parts' division for all the early bits and bobs
departures? Let's hope Lucifer's keeping an inventory.
Otherwise all our losses are thrown in together – drawers
rolling with missing marbles, chests heaving with stifled
sounds and stunted visions, cast off statures jostling in
wardrobes like outsized suits! It's a strenuous affair, this
dying – as bad as being born – but flecked through with an
awful kind of . . . conscience. I suppose your mother sent
you to cast the first stone.

Marta   I got your address from the Embassy. My mother's
dead. She died in April.

Denis   Oh.

Several beats.

Husband? You have a husband?

Marta   No.

Denis   Children?

Marta   Not yet.

Denis   She was twenty years younger, more. I was fifty, she
was twenty-seven. Heart attack, was it?

Marta   An embolism.

Denis   Good for her. None of this limping around the bush,
dying piecemeal. That's my problem – the heart's too strong,
genuine German engineering on your great grandfather's
side, doesn't know when to quit . . . Tea, you'll have tea?

You'll have to make it yourself, I'm afraid, if you can find a clean cup. Or I can call up the Castle Arms, ask them to deliver something. They sometimes do if they're not too busy – I kept that place in business once upon a time. I filled every en-suite with embassy guests. They owe me!

Marta   She said you beat her.

Denis   What?

Marta   My mother said she was six months pregnant with me. You took her to your summer house in the mountains. To relax you said. Then you took the gas pipe from the cooker and you beat her with it. You beat her so bad she almost lost me . . .

Several beats. He seems stricken by the possibility – or memory – of it but quickly recovers. He goes to the phone table, consults his book of numbers.

Denis   'C' . . . Cathy, Cristophe, Canadian Consul, Carmelites, Chilean Embassy, Christchurch tours, Carlos, Crematorium, Constantina, Celia Suarez . . .

He halts, puzzled.

What is it I'm looking for?

He sees the yellow Post-it with her name on it.

Oh yes. 'Marta'. 'Marvellous Marta' . . . It helps if I add an alliterative. 'Jolly James', 'Cantankerous Constantina', 'Lovely Lupita', 'Marvellous Marta' . . .

He adds 'Marvellous' to 'Marta' on the Post-it, notices the time.

Ten past five! Twenty minutes before the post office closes. We'd better get going. You drive, I hope? I specifically asked for a home-help who does. Wait there, it's Marta, my little girl's birthday next week, I have to post her something. It's a jewellery box belonging to my mother. My grandfather carved it for her when she was a child. I think she'll like it.

She doesn't answer.

Denis   Just a second, I'll get it. It's already wrapped.

Denis *goes off to search for the jewellery box. While he's gone* **Marta** *looks through the photographs on the mantelpiece, takes the one of the little girl he thought was her and leaves.*

Denis *returns with the box.*

Denis   Here it is. Strange . . . It's already got stamps on it – Bolivian stamps . . . What does that say?

He pushes the box away from himself long-sightedly.

Denis   'Devolver Al Remitente'? What date is that? What does it say?

Marta, *he notices, has gone. He looks about the empty room in bewilderment, notices the yellow Post-it of 'Marvellous Marta' stuck to his sleeve.*

Denis   Marta . . . Marta?

Scene Four

Kay *is reading in bed.* **Alan** *enters.*

Alan   Morning.

She doesn't react. He goes out and does it again – bigger.

Alan   Morning!

Same result – he goes for a third time – huge.

Alan   I said 'good mor –'

Kay   I heard you! And noted the pantomime.

Alan   Excellent! I exist. I'm not just a fiction of my own imagination. I had a little existential crisis there in the kitchen – a Mr Sellophane moment. I suppose subsidence affects people too, not just buildings, if somebody cuts the ground from under them . . .

Kay   Good. He's picking on you for a change.

Alan   Not Myles – her, the niñera.

Kay   The 'niñera' has a name.

Alan   She was standing at the sink scratching her back with one of the little bone-handled dessert forks we got in Fez. 'Buenos Días' I said, in case she didn't hear me come in. She didn't flinch, didn't so much as turn to acknowledge me. She just stood there, bra-less and barefoot, until she'd satisfied her itch and then, do you know what she did? Knowing I was watching? She put it back in the drawer. She put the fork she'd relieved herself with back in the drawer without even wiping the damn thing!

Kay   You have a hissy fit when anyone washes those forks. You say it degrades the bone.

Alan   That's not the point, is it? Well, instead of slinking out with my Rennie like a dismissed servant, I had the audacity to stay and make myself a French Roast.

Kay   Yes, I smelt it . . . I thought you were off caffeine?

Alan   I needed something noisy. The kettle seemed a bit meek. She'd moved on to my *Guardian* at this point. Lounging on the couch with her feet against the wall and the supplements across her lap . . .

Kay   That's when you noticed the bra-lessness, was it?

Alan   What?

Kay   You could have brought me a coffee . . .

Alan   I had to plug it out before it finished. It's embarrassing, the sounds a percolator makes, especially in that atmosphere . . . She probably thought it was my intestines protesting after last night's curry, and of course the tell-tale Rennie. What do you think I've done?

Kay   Thank God. The honeymoon is over at last. Like my Dad used to say, the best cure for a crush is constant exposure to the cause of it.

Alan   What honeymoon? (*Getting dressed.*) She asked me
about the novel yesterday, 'What's it about?' she demanded.
I told her my wife wouldn't ask me that!

Kay   I don't have to, unfortunately the news bulletins from
the frontline are all too frequent . . .

Alan   I explained that to a writer that is the most reductive,
the most intrusive, the most unhelpful question a person can
ask. And that if a novel is any good at all, it's about the eighty
thousand words it takes to write it.

Kay   You actually said that?

Alan   No, but I will do if she has the cheek to ask again.
Why can't people mind their own business? Or write their
own damn novel if they're so interested! Forty-seven
thousand eight hundred and sixty-something last word
count. I'm over half way. Of course it's rough . . . But no
rougher than one would expect of a first draft. Do you
remember that architect in Venice? The one with the
wife with the botched boob job – a chip on both shoulders
you said.

Kay   Oh yes, the couple in the room with the balcony – the
one we should have got.

Alan   He said he always judged a book by its length, not its
cover. That he didn't read anything that didn't fit into his
jeans pocket and that usually fell between seventy and ninety
thousand words.

Kay (*remembering*)   'The snug fit novel.'

Alan   You agreed with him.

Kay   I humoured him. He was intimidated – the whole
'novelist' thing . . . He'd have lain awake all night rehearsing
something clever to say at the breakfast buffet. Don't bully
Marta, the kids love her. Claire told me yesterday she wants
to look exactly like Marta when she grows up. And Myles has
even taken to washing himself.

Alan With remarkable vigour, I've noticed . . . Did he do that?

He notices the bruise on her arm.

Kay Your son has set a new record for wrestling his mother to the floor. One point four seconds – with Marta watching.

Alan You shouldn't let him do that. Myles needs you to act like his mother, not the family Alsatian.

Kay I got him back. Crept up on him while he was texting and caught him right in the back of the knees. He went down like a sack of flour – whoomph!

Her phone sounds. She reads it.

Nine thirty is cancelled – damn! It was a second viewing, the wife was already planning her window-boxes and the husband urinated not just once but twice along the boundary wall . . . I'll take the kids to training.

Alan And leave me alone with her? Not a chance. Even now, as we speak, she's defiling the Culture section. Why a person can't turn a page without spitting on the corner of it is beyond me. I'm going to call the agency once it opens.

Kay And do what?

Alan I can't write in a curdled atmosphere!

Kay Asking what your novel is about is hardly grounds for a dismissal.

Alan Typical! Go on! Deliberately misconstrue and ridicule everything I say!

Kay If you're ever going to publish this thing, you're going to have to learn how to talk about it. I can't sell a property without offering some kind of description.

Alan A 'description' is another matter entirely – you're never asked what a house is 'about'. What's this four-bedroom imitation-Georgian family residence with a south-facing conservatory and planning permission for a detached granny cottage which, given your mother is dead and mine is courting the prospect, we're unlikely to ever use *about*? Well?

Kay (*getting out of bed*)   That certainly does sound like your intestines rumbling. Did you take that Rennie?

Alan   Ha-bloody-ha.

She moves into the bathroom off where we hear a tap running.

By the way, what do you mean '*if* I'm ever going to publish this *thing* . . .' I'll arrange for Myles and Claire to publish it posthumously if need be!

He paces the floor, distracted by the subject of his novel.

Actually the forty-seven thousand eight hundred and sixty-three words are reading a bit 'thin'. I've tried to beef it up by introducing the saucy Latina nanny who scratches her mole with the family silver and scoffs her take-out chow mein with the wife's Indonesian hairpins.

Sound of tooth-paste spat. **Kay** *re-enters, toothbrush in hand, foam around her lips.*

Kay   How do you know?

Beat.

In the centre of her back, where the bra-strap you noticed wasn't there irritates it, she has a mole. How did you come by that little 'observation'?

Alan   A reasonable guess? A writer's intuition of meaningless detail? I assume she hasn't got fleas – What are you suggesting?

Kay   Your mother warned me. She said I shouldn't let another woman into the house who still had her own teeth. 'It's as second nature as a dog lifting his leg on a lamp-post', is how she put it.

Alan   Since when has my mother become the oracle of domestic bliss? My father nurtured his own cancer to get away from her!

Kay   Don't gaslight me. When did you see Marta using my hairpins as chopsticks?

Alan   I didn't –

Kay   You just said.

Alan   I was elaborating on the fiction of the mole –

Kay   The most vividly imagined mole . . .

Alan   I'm a dermatologist, for Christ's sake! How do *you* know about the mole? If there even is one . . .

Kay   The skin-doctor-turned-novelist, your license to fuck her one way or another.

Alan   What?

Kay   You admitted she was attractive. Four weeks in, after the trial period, we were lying in bed and I asked you 'Do you think she's attractive'? You said 'Do I think who's attractive?'

Alan   How does that constitute an admission?

Kay   Oh please. The evasion was all the more telling.

Alan   We agreed she wasn't attractive before we hired her.

Kay   Keep your voice down. We agreed she wasn't 'beautiful'.

Alan (*amazed*)   You're jealous! I suppose I should be flattered. To be rewarded for a crime I didn't even commit!

Kay   You thought about it, admit it.

Alan   I think about all fictional possibilities. That's what I do – when I'm not taking care of our children, that is.

Kay   Go ahead. Have your head fuck. Just don't imagine it's anything other than the cliché it is.

Kay *exits.* **Alan** *shouts after her.*

Alan   You didn't answer my question, I notice! How do *you* know about the mole? Well? Clearly someone else has a keen interest in what's lurking under the nanny's bra-strap!

He hears a door slam. **Alan** *stands adrift for a moment, then grabs the back of a property-sales brochure, fumbles for a pen in the bedside locker and begins writing.*

Scene Five

Denis *is sitting on the edge of his bed in his pyjamas, his formerly oiled hair a wisp of fluff about his head. His home help,* **Bernadette**, *a matronly woman in her fifties, chooses his clothes from the wardrobe, before peeling off his pyjama top.*

Bernie   Up your arms, oopsy daisy!

Denis   Don't 'oopsy daisy' me – I'm not a child.

She whisks his vest over his head, puts on a clean one. His arms remain stretched in a surrender gesture above his head.

Bernie   Down again. Good man. Tip forward for me . . .

He tips forward, she dresses him in a clean shirt.

Denis   I'm not your 'good man' either. Otherwise I wouldn't have to suffer strangers' hands pawing and poking me . . . Ow! What's your name again?

Bernie   Bernadette. Bernie, if it's easier.

Denis   How would it be 'easier'? I can remember or forget two syllabels as easily as three. 'Bernadette from Bray . . .' It's easier if I can put something with it. Ravishing Roberta, Devilish Donna, Braying Bernadette . . .

While she's choosing trousers for him he reaches for another yellow Post-it pad. The headboard and surrounds are covered in them.

Bernie   Balbriggan actually.

Denis   What?

Bernie   Who's Marvellous Marta? Another one of your admirers?

She shows the yellow Post-it stuck to the bottom of his shoe.

Denis   Put that back! There. On the locker beside the bank statement so I can remember. On the envelope. Not like that – I won't see it, will I, if the envelope is shut!

Beat.

How many have you?

Bernie   How many what – Dastardly Denises giving me guff?

Denis   Offspring, litter. Quite a few by the look of it . . .

He watches her ample hindquarters.

Bernie   I have an army of two sons, four daughters and seven strapping grandchildren so you better behave yourself. Hold onto me.

She supports him to standing onto his Zimmer frame.

You've a few chips off the old block yourself, I notice. None of them living local?

Denis   Not local, no.

Bernie   Lucky you. Sometimes I think himself and myself should feck off to Florida, leave them to mind their own children. Up your foot . . . and the other . . .? Off we pop!

She removes the underpants and pyjama bottoms, slips on clean pants and trousers.

Denis   They'll look after you, I suppose?

Bernie   I can look after myself, thank you very much.

Denis   When you can't – when the bits of you are 'off we popping' ahead of the rest. I found two toe nails in my slipper yesterday, the only surprise was the toes weren't attached. And it's not dandruff that's left in my hat now but my entire scalp – skin, hair – the lot!

Bernie   I wouldn't worry, with that big block you've plenty to spare.

Denis   You don't think it will happen to you? You think you'll stop like a clock in your sleep, or shuffle off the pavement in front of a bus? They're the lucky ones – the ones who have someone to give them a push in the path of a double-decker, the son or daughter who sees you sleeping with a smile on your face and applies a pillow to keep it there . . . You can't pay people to do that! Not in this bloody country!

Bernie   My lot will wring me dry . . . Throw me in a home or something . . .

Denis   Children. Grandchildren. There's your ticket to a Swiss clinic!

She buckles him into his trousers.

Bernie   No more gloom and doom from you – you'll have an egg? A nice poached egg with a bit of toast?

Denis   What time is it?

Bernie   Ten more minutes and I'm fecking off.

Denis   We don't have time for breakfast, we'd better hurry. You can drop me there if necessary – I'll get a taxi back.

Bernie   A taxi back from where?

Denis   The post office on the Green. I have business to take care of.

Bernie   Sorry your excellency, I'm not authorised to drop you anywhere.

Denis   Well, I'm authorising you. I need to get to the post office today – now – while I have my wits about me.

Bernie   Maybe tomorrow.

Denis   Tomorrow's Sunday. The post office doesn't open on a Sunday.

Bernie   Monday then.

Denis   I could be dead by Monday.

Bernie   Don't be morbid.

Denis   I'm not being morbid. I'm being bloody optimistic.

She tidies away his clothes.

Denis   I'll pay you time and a half. Double!

Bernie   We can't accept cash from clients – it's an agency rule. Families think we're trying to diddle them out of their inheritance. Anyway, I don't have a car.

Denis   You don't have a . . . I asked, I *specified* that I needed someone with their own transport!

Bernie   I have the bicycle out back. That'd be a good one – Bernie from the Towers peddling up the Green with the former Ambassador on her bar. I like the sound of that, be nearly worth getting fired for. I'll make you that egg. You can eat it or turn your imperial backside to it.

As she leaves, **Denis** *reaches for the telephone on the locker, knocks the glass jug of water onto the floor, shattering it.*

Bernie   Now look what you've done!

Denis   I need to call a taxi to bring me to the post office.

Bernie   You'll be paying me overtime alright but not to carry you to the post!

Denis   It's her birthday next week. I need to send something. Money, I suppose. No child would object to money? I sent her a jewellery box once – the genuine article – antique bog oak, hard-carved with a what's-it, a . . . tutu . . . twisting . . . slippers . . . ballerina! A ballerina inside but she sent it back. Or the mother did. Lupita. Loop de Loopita. Are all women bad, do you think? Or do I bring out the worst in them?

Bernie   Like attracts like they say. Move your feet.

He reaches to pick up the broken jug.

Bernie Leave it! You'll hurt yourself.

Denis 'The hose pipe from the gas cooker . . .' We didn't even have gas . . . It was what's-it – that awful smell – paraffin . . . Used to blacken everything . . .

He reaches for the block of yellow Post-its – then a pen. She nudges him back onto the bed.

Bernie Sit there! Don't move! I'll get a dust pan and brush . . .

He reaches again for the pen to write on his Post-it.

Bernie What did I say?

Denis Roll over, play dead . . .

Bernie Not on my shift, I've two grandchildren waiting for their supper. What are you going to do?

Denis 'Sit'.

Bernie Good man.

She leaves. He sits stock still. After a while the phone rings. He doesn't dare to move to attempt to answer it.

Scene Six

Marta *in the kitchen, dialling a number on her phone. She waits, gets an answering machine.* **Kay** *disturbs her. She is carrying a briefcase, a hectic pile of papers and a bottle of champagne – all of which she dumps onto the table. She's already a little tipsy as we shall see.*

Kay Sorry I'm late . . . I managed to offload this ghastly lump of a house for double its asking and quarter its worth.

Marta A sale?

Kay   More than a sale, it was beautiful – it was a fucking work of art. We had the asking in hand weeks ago – the vendor couldn't believe his luck. Just short of a million for a white elephant he'd received in lieu of a gambling debt of seventy grand a decade ago. Of course he wanted to seize it immediately. Grab his loot and run. The other agents were the same – there were three of us sharing the commission – the other two pussies wanted to dash out and lodge the deposit and slap a 'Sale Agreed' on it quick before the buyer woke up and smelled his first mortgage payment. But I had a hunch . . . The first client I'd shown it to – a fat man with psoriasis and a greasy suit. He'd played his cards close to his chest, scarcely looked at the house. Just looked at the site – two acres – asked about planning restrictions in the area, whether being a period property there was a protection order on it.

'Wait,' I told the vendor, 'sit tight. It ain't over 'til the fat man sings . . .' And he did. Just as the vendor was panicking our buyer would see something decent and pull – in comes his bid, one point two million. That's when the bottle of Bollinger was bought. I kept it corked, went back to the first bidder. He was raging – not so much at the loss of the house but that someone else had knocked him down a rung, climbed ahead of him on the property ladder. That's when he started bidding with his ego instead of his cheque book.

Marta   That's horrible. How can you enjoy making someone pay more than they can afford for what – a piece of shit –

Kay   Ah! It's not over – not yet. Mr Desperado very kindly drove the price up to one point seven at which point he tucked his tail between his legs, departed from the table and left the fat cat to pay the bill. It was perfect. Our one-of-a-kind crumbling period property will be demolished in – I give it three months, six at the outside while he passes the brown envelope and pulls the various strings. Then, you watch, he'll be stashing the profits, I'll have the selling of a 'luxurious complex of two and three bed apartments'. (*Pops the cork of the champagne.*) Win win.

Kay *pours two glasses of champagne, passes one to* **Marta**.

Kay   What shall we drink to?

Marta   You don't want to wait until Alan gets down?

Kay   Coq au vin – my husband's favourite . . . You've been busy . . .

Marta   I relieved Alan. He was distracted.

Kay   I bet he was . . . Where is the budding Booker-winner?

Marta   In his bedroom, I think.

Kay *puts the champagne in the fridge, notices the painting on the door of it – an eleven-year-old's family portrait of what seems like the parents and children in the foreground, and a large Jeep driving out of the frame.*

Kay   Either I look flatteringly like you or I'm conspicuously absent from my daughter's family portrait.

Marta   That's you in the Jeep. At least, that's your hand waving goodbye. You're going to work, she said.

Beat.

He printed the first draft of his novel today. It's very brave.

Kay   Let you read it, did he?

Marta   No, I mean that he does it. Gives up a good job, takes care of his kids, writes his book . . .

Kay   I would defer judgement on the latter until I'd read it if I were you. (*Removing shoes.*) Ow! We should be wearing pocket-sprung, dynamo-powered, miniature BMWs on our feet, not this prehistoric shit. Do you know what this bone-crunching harpoon says about female elv-evolution?

Kay *rubs her feet; displays the culprit – a heeled court shoe.*

Marta   It says you're drunk.

Kay   It says we're fucked. We're all fucked, one way
or another.

Marta   You didn't drive, did you?

Kay   No, I did not drive, even though I was quite capable
of it, I took a taxi. Eighty quid the greedy bastard charged
me – just because he saw the bottle in Bollie in my bag. Don't
tell Alan. He doesn't mind me getting drunk but he does get
anxious about me spending money. Note the dented cans of
Batchelors beans in the pantry, my penny-pinching husband
would knock down a dozen Eastern Europeans to bag a
bargain. Who's that? Not Alan?

Sound of a Spanish guitar overhead.

Marta   Myles asked if he could borrow my guitar, he's been
on YouTube all evening taking lessons. He's very talented.

Kay   He's very smitten . . .

Marta (*absent-mindedly scratching her back with a
chopstick*)   'Smitten'?

Kay   It's a household condition the origin of which
coincides with your arrival. (*Taking the chopstick from* **Marta**.)
You should let Alan take a look at that mole. He used to be a
skin doctor. Before, that is, he realised that treating other
people's itches was merely a distraction from satisfying
his own.

Marta   I'm sorry that you find your husband ridiculous.

Several beats. **Kay** *stakes her escaping hair with the confiscated
chopstick.*

Kay   I never said my husband was ridiculous. I simply don't
feel compelled to get down on bended knee to worship a
man who chooses to pack his children's lunchboxes. (*About
the fridge portrait again.*) Claire has drawn you in the middle
of her and her father, holding each of their hands . . . What
does the child psychologist have to say about that?

Marta   I'm glad that your daughter likes me. I like your children very much.

Kay   That's very disciplined of you – after six months. I'd better warn you, my 'likeable' family has a whopping great crush on you. We can try to hide it, but there it is in coloured crayon. Look, Claire has painted love-hearts escaping from the chimney – the entire house is smoking with lust for nanny.

Beat.

Don't worry. I'm not jealous. I look at you and do you know what I see? I see the mirror image of everything I'd rather have than be. You're the cloth I went to great lengths to cut myself out of. Marta Morales, my surrogate wife, my children's substitute Mommy.

Marta   'Surrogate wife'? You want me to mind your kids *and* fuck your husband?

The phone rings. **Kay** *picks up.*

Kay   Yes?

She listens, passes the phone to **Marta**.

Kay   The Bolivian Embassy . . .

Marta (*on the phone*)   Diga . . . Sí, soy you, Marta . . . No, nadie me informó . . . ¿Cuándo ocurrió? ¿Ha sido enterrado ya? Bueno, gracias, gracias por avisarme . . .

She sets aside the phone. **Kay** *registers the altered mood.*

Kay   Bad news?

Marta   He's dead. They buried him almost a month ago.

Kay   Someone you knew?

Marta   No, not someone I knew. My father.

The pot boils over behind **Marta**. *She tends to it.*

Kay   I'm sorry.

She lays a tentative hand on **Marta**'s *back.*

Marta   What for?

Kay   I . . .

Beat.

My husband has been pretending not to notice how
attractive you are.

Marta *turns and kisses* **Kay**, *an emphatic kiss that catches* **Kay** *off-guard but not unwilling.*

Marta   Does that make you feel safer?

Several beats as **Kay** *recovers.* **Marta** *brings the pots to the table.*

Marta   Myles! Claire! Venga, a la mesa! Ninos? Is no one in
this house hungry?

Alan *enters.*

Alan   Something smells good!

Kay   Yes it does . . .

Alan   Kids will be down in a sec – Myles is on the phone
and I sent Claire to the bathroom to scrub up. Anything I
can do?

Kay (*slight slur*)   I doubt it – Marta seems to have everything
in hand . . . Excuse me while I 'slip into something less
comfortable' . . .

Alan (*surprised*)   You're drunk.

Kay   Yes I am, and I intend to get a great deal drunker.

Alan   For God's sake. Try not to make it obvious to the
children that you're . . .

Kay   That I'm what? Their mother? Not just a cash
machine with a three-letter PIN that says M-U-M instead
of D-A-D ?

Alan (*after her as she exits*)   Glad you remembered, I thought
you'd mistaken us for a laundry stop!

Marta *and* **Alan** *are left alone.*

Alan   Sorry about that. She's insufferable when she closes a deal – makes her even cockier than usual . . . Kids don't mind too much, do they, not at Claire and Myles's age, they seem to think seeing their mother intoxicated is marvellous entertainment. (*The champagne.*) Is that yours?

Marta   Kay poured it for me.

Alan   Good. Good for you. You're off-duty. (*Checking the clock – ten to.*) Just about . . . Salud!

Marta   I'll help Claire clean up . . .

Marta *wipes her hands on the tea towel, is about to exit. He gestures to the oven.*

Alan   That okay like that? I shouldn't turn it down or . . . The top gets a good deal hotter than you might expect, be a shame if it spoiled or –

Marta   The temperature's fine, it's as it should be . . .

Alan (*roots in the freezer*)   I'll just pop a few nuggets in the oven for Claire and Myles. They may not be too keen on the old 'vin' in the 'coq' . . .

Marta   It's perfectly safe for children. The alcohol evaporates.

Alan   Oh I know, it's just the taste. Neither of them are very adventurous, I'm afraid . . .

Marta *watches him for several beats as he rattles nuggets and oven chips onto a baking tray. There's a territorial quality to both the action and the attitude that's hard to ignore.*

Alan   I'll make them a carrot and apple salad as well. Clock up another two of their five a day . . .

Marta *follows* **Kay** *upstairs. As* **Alan** *is grating carrots and chopping apples, we see* **Marta** *pass the open bedroom door where* **Kay** *is inside changing. They look at each other a moment.* **Marta** *hesitates;* **Kay** *pulls her in and closes the door behind her.*

Lights out. Interval if there is one.

Scene Seven

Kay and Alan's bedroom, late morning, many 'mornings' later. Kay lying in Marta's lap, with Marta combing through Kay's glorious hair with her fingers as Kay checks her phone messages, deleting and saving as appropriate.

Marta   My mother had hair like yours . . . I used to comb it for her . . .

Kay   Oh dear . . . what does that mean – you're having an affair with your mother substitute?

Marta   You're nothing like my mother. She was a very timid woman. I don't think she ever got over the shock of my father. It was like being run over by a juggernaut.

Kay   Poor man . . .

Marta   Poor 'man'?!

Kay   Yes, I feel sorry for them – men who spend their lives with women who make them feel like bulls in china shops. It's not honest. A woman is always stronger than a man. If she lets him think otherwise it's bound to backfire . . .

Marta   That's not true, that's ridiculous . . .

Kay   Is it? Every man I've ever met, you let them know who's boss – they might throw a few shapes to begin with – but hold the line and even the biggest lions are purring like kittens in no time. (*On the phone.*) Hi Paul, I'm delayed at a property, you'll have to take the rest of my viewings . . . No, just the morning, I'll be in by two. Great. Thanks. (*Phone off; at* **Marta**'s *'look'.*) What?

Marta   If you were a man, I could quite cheerfully hate you . . .

Kay   Good. I'm not planning a sex-change anytime soon . . .

Marta   You don't need to. If your inner man got any bigger, it would be like unleashing King Kong!

Kay   Thank you, I'll take that as a compliment . . .

They kiss, begin to make love. **Kay** *'tops'* **Marta** *but* **Marta** *flips her.*

Marta   Ah. You can't be boss on the street and between the sheets, that's very, very bad for you . . . Lie still.

Marta *pins* **Kay***'s wrists above her head and ties them to the bedpost with the scrunchy (***Kay***'s) from around her wrist.*

Kay   King Kong restrained by a hair tie, who would have thought [it] –

Marta   Shh! (*Kisses her silent.*) Where do you keep your stockings?

Kay   It should be chains, we could use the chain from Myles's mountain bike –

Marta (*silencing her with another kiss*)   No chains. Even Houdini couldn't have escaped from a woman's stockings . . . Now where are they?

Kay   By the window. Top drawer.

Marta *gets the stockings and secures* **Kay***'s feet to each post of the bed.*

Kay   We don't have much time. I have viewings at two and Alan gets back from his writers' group at three –

Marta   Shhh! No more 'Alan'. Not while I'm making love to you . . .

Marta *straddles* **Kay***, pulls* **Kay***'s vest over her eyes so it acts as a blindfold. She reaches for the matches on the locker, cracks one.*

Kay   You're making me nervous.

Marta   Good.

She lights a tapered candle with the match, lets the wax burn a little before holding it high above **Kay***'s body and letting a drop fall.*

Kay   Ow!

Marta   Too much?

Kay   Yes! No . . . Do it again.

Marta   'Please'.

Kay   Please . . .

Marta *traces a line of wax drops from* **Kay**'s *chest towards her navel. Then she dips her fingers in the glass of water on the locker and runs her wet fingertips over* **Kay**'s *torso to her navel.*

Kay   That's good, that's . . . Oh . . .

Marta's *hand disappears under the sheet over* **Kay**'s *hips.* **Kay** *stops talking, giving way to a series of murmurs as* **Marta**'s *hand moves under the sheet.*

Kay   Inside . . .

Marta   Inside – what?

Kay   'Please . . .'

Marta *obliges. They don't immediately hear a car pull up outside; they do, however, hear the front door shut some beats later.*

Kay   Fuck!

Marta   It couldn't be, he's never early, he's always –

Alan (*off*)   Kay . . . ? Kay! You home?

Kay   Shit!

They hear him walk through the rooms below, then amble up the stairs as they frantically untie **Kay**'s *wrists. He's on the stairs now.*

Kay   Get in the bathroom, quick! In!

Marta *dashes into the ensuite bathroom leaving* **Kay** *with both feet still tied.* **Kay** *manages to untie one, then throw the quilt over the post with the foot still tied to it and lie back in the bed as if sleeping before* **Alan** *enters.*

Alan   Damn writers' group was cancelled. The room was double-booked and of course the bloody Quakers got it – What's wrong? What are you doing in bed? I thought you had appointments all day –

Kay   I wasn't feeling great. I grabbed a breakfast roll on my way in to the office, the sausages must have been a bit off . . .

Alan   You sick? That's a first. I'd say you've got yourself a temperature too – you look flushed.

He sits on the bed, feels her temperature. His sitting on the quilt dislodges it so that the stocking tie on the bedpost is just showing.

Kay   I'm fine. I just need to sleep it off . . .

Alan   Where did you get the roll?

Kay   What?

Alan   The breakfast roll that poisoned you, who sold you it?

Kay   Oh . . . That place on the roundabout – the garage. If it even was the roll, I was feeling a bit . . . iffy . . .

Alan   We should bloody sue them! Imagine – offloading rotten sausages on a customer that fills their Jeep three times a week!

Kay   If I could just have some quiet –

Alan   It could be a twenty-four hour thing. Quite a few of the children at school had it last week. I'll get you a cold cloth.

He moves towards the bathroom; she grabs him. The action exposes the remaining tied foot more.

Kay   No! (*softer*) I – I don't want anything. Just . . . (*thinks*) If you could get me a glass of milk from the kitchen. Or toast. Some dried toast to settle my stomach. That would be perfect. Thanks . . .

He looks at her. Her behaviour is odd.

Alan   Probably best if you steered clear of the kids this evening, just to be on the safe side. I'll tell them to leave you alone until we're sure it's not infectious –

He notices the stocking tied to the bedpost, traces it to **Kay**'s *attached foot.*

Alan   What's this?

Kay   It's nothing. It's just . . .

Alan   How does tying your foot to the bedpost help with food poisoning?

Kay   It's not . . . It's . . . Go to the kitchen and make some toast – please.

He surveys the scene with a new dawning perspective, eyes the bathroom door, tries the handle, it's locked.

Alan   Who's in there?

Kay (*trying to undo the tie*)   Please Alan, I'm doing you a favour. Go out and come back in a hour like you were fucking supposed to.

Alan (*banging on the bathroom door*)   Who the fuck is in there? Who?

He grabs **Kay** *by the shoulders.*

Kay   Get off me!

They hear the door unlock behind him. **Marta** *emerges from the bathroom dressed in what she pulled out of the laundry basket.*

Alan *is relieved – briefly . . .*

Alan   Marta? Why didn't you say it was just . . . (*penny dropping*) Marta . . .

Marta (*to* **Kay**)   You okay?

Alan   That's my shirt. Why is she wearing my shirt . . .

Kay (*to* **Marta**)   Go. Take the Jeep.

Kay *passes her the keys from her jacket pocket on the floor.* **Marta** *hesitates.*

Kay   Marta. Please. Get out of here.

Marta *leaves.* **Kay** *pulls on her clothes.*

Alan (*reeling*)   Our children's . . . You and our . . . (*Several beats.*) She's got to go, there's no question of her staying on now –

Kay   Alan –

Alan (*reaching for the phone on the locker*)   I'm calling the agency. Tell them she's not safe – to think we let her into our home, let her into our family – I'm getting a restraining order, a barring order – whatever – I don't want that bitch in heat near my children again –

Kay   Alan! This has nothing to do with the agency. Marta and I like each other. A great deal . . .

Alan   We all 'liked' Marta 'a great deal', that doesn't mean we let her tie us to the bedposts! How long has this been going on? Days? Weeks? What have you been doing – sneaking home to screw the help while I'm taxiing our children to school?

Kay   Oh for Christ's . . .

Alan   What do you think I am – the mug that takes care of our children while you're at home playing Mulholland Drive with their nanny! You hated that film by the way, you said you failed to see how two women could achieve orgasms by swishing their hair and air-kissing each other's shoulders!

Kay   I am not going to stand here and entertain you with the details . . .

Alan   What about the children? Have they seen you? Claire and Myles better not have seen you two –

Kay   Of course they haven't 'seen' us. Let's not talk now. We'll discuss things later when everyone's calmer. Then we can come to some kind of civilised arrangement.

Alan   'Civilised' – what's that? I get a slice of the action too? Mommy and Daddy both get to fuck the nanny?

Kay   You prick . . .

Alan (*laughing*)   Oh that's good . . . Coming from someone who's just fucked her children's nanny, that is just priceless . . . (*Deadly serious.*) Don't think for one minute I'm going to just disappear and let the two of you play happy families . . . That is not the deal here, that is so not the deal!

Kay *is about to leave.*

Alan   Where do you think you're going?

Kay   I'm going to work to earn your bloody alimony. I'll be back about nine – when the kids are in bed. I presume you can manage without childcare till then . . .

She exits, leaving **Alan** *alone in the bedroom reeling.*

Scene Eight

Lights up on **Alan** *at the kitchen sink, filling a glass of water, waiting for his Solpadeine to dissolve.*

He watches **Kay** *enter the living room area. She is hauling a large suitcase into which she quickly packs a few select folders from the shelf before continuing to gather and collect the rest of her things.*

Alan   Don't forget this one. Marta's I believe. 'Biological Exuberance: Animal Homosexuality and Natural Diversity.' I borrowed it – purely for research purposes, mind, although I imagine there are those less-experienced readers who might use it as a kind of instruction manual.

*She comes to take it but he whisks it out of her reach.**

Alan   'Bonobos have one of the most varied and extensive repertoires of homosexual practice found in any animal. Females engage in an extraordinary form of mutual genital stimulation that, in many aspects, is unique to their species –' Not so, it seems, not so . . . 'Sometimes known as GG-rubbing (for genito-genital rubbing), this behaviour is usually performed in a face-to-face embracing position . . .

---

* The following extracts are taken from *Biological Exuberance* © 1999 by Bruce Bagemihl. Reprinted by permission of St. Martin's Press. All rights reserved.

One female stands on all fours and literally carries or lifts her partner off the ground; the female on the bottom wraps her legs around the other's waist and clings to her as they rapidly rub their genitals against one another, directly stimulating each other's clitoris. As shown by their facial expressions, vocalisations, and genital engorgement, females experience intense pleasure – and probably orgasm – during homosexual interactions . . . They grimace or "grin" by baring their teeth wide and also utter screams or squeals that are thought to be associated with sexual climax . . .' Ah! And there was me thinking you'd left the kettle on the Aga.

Kay   I'm glad you find all this amusing.

Alan   More than amusing, it's hilarious – informative too. Did you know that orangs are partial to a little GG action too? 'Lesbian activity in orangs usually involves one female fondling the genitals of another female, often inserting her fingers, thumbs and other digits, into the vagina of the other. Sometimes she also masturbates herself with her foot while she is penetrating the other female'! With her own foot, imagine! I bet you wish you'd kept up that yoga.

Kay   You're disgusting.

Alan   Me? You're calling me disgusting? I'm merely sharing the Kama Sutra of your bestial brethren . . . Where were we? Oh yes, Hanuman langurs, I believe I underlined something . . . ah, here we are . . . 'All females participate freely in homosexual mounting, including lactating, pregnant, menstruating, ovulating and nonovulating females. This behaviour is especially common' – hark – 'especially common among mothers, who have developed a special "baby-sitting" system. They transfer their young to other individuals in the troop (usually female but sometimes male)' – in your case, to me, the father – 'this allows them to engage in homosexual (and other) activities . . .' I might have to translate this – it's not written in a very child-friendly style. Still, it will be useful for Claire and Myles to know that their mother is not entirely alone in the animal kingdom . . .

Kay *tries to snatch the book out of his hands, a scuffle ensues during which* **Marta** *enters.*

Marta   Get your hands off her.

Kay   It's okay, the book he's preaching from isn't his.

Alan   Marta! How good of you to join us. We've been discussing the social bonding techniques of your animal kin – GG-rubbing bonobos, fanny-footing orangs, child-abandoning langurs – my, what an exuberant planet we're living on. The children will be delighted to know their mother is joining a veritable lesbian utopia out there among the gang-banging sage grouse and black stilts. Oh, and the militant orange-fronted parakeets. Listen to this, I'm sure you'll identify: 'Some female couples successfully compete against heterosexual pairs for nesting sites; pair-bonded females often become powerful allies that support one another and may even come to dominate opposite-sex pairs through attacks and threat behaviour'.

Kay   You haven't seen the beginning of 'threat behaviour'. If you lay any of that crap on the children . . .

Alan   What? What are you going to do? Explain to them Mommy has a Bonobo Complex?

Marta   Come on, let's go, don't get involved.

Alan   Fine, go, walk out that door, don't flatter yourself you'll be missed.

Kay   We'll collect the children once I've found a place for us to live.

Alan (*to* **Marta**)   Our daughter wouldn't have survived her uterus if it weren't for me. Didn't she tell you? She spent the first four months wanting to abort her.

Kay (*winded*)   You shit. You low, cowardly, selfish piece of shit.

Marta   Ignore him, Kay. This isn't helping.

Alan   What isn't helping is you grooming my children and screwing their mother!

Marta   Let's go . . .

He bars **Marta**'s *exit.*

Alan   Where else did you fuck her? Besides our bed, our children's? Did you fuck her in our children's beds?

Kay   Get out of her way.

Marta   I don't want to fight with you.

Alan   Fine. Let's discuss it then – like three two-legged mammals. I want to know where you fucked my wife!

Kay   *I* fucked *her* on the couch, the armchair and against the mudroom door – both sides. The first time was in the kitchen. She sat on the table with her feet braced against the fridge. I wiped the print off before the children came home from tennis. Where were you? Oh yes, at one of your writers' groups. Discussing the latest manual you'd discovered on creative writing – 'The Wild Mind' . . .

She laughs.

Alan   Get out. Get out of my house!

Kay   'Your' house? It's my name on the deeds. I pay the mortgage.

Marta   Let's go. Now.

Alan   What are you going to do? Turf me and my children onto the street?

Kay   We'll discuss practical arrangements about *our* children when you're capable of speaking without spitting.

Alan   Marvellous! Meanwhile I'll tell Myles and Claire that their mother is experiencing a mid-life crisis, also known in zoological terms as 'an excess of biological exuberance'. And that after she's raised her leg on all the items of furniture she can reach, she'll be back mewling at the back door, lifting her tail for forgiveness!

Kay *leaves.* **Alan** *grabs* **Marta**'s *arm.*

Alan   You do realise you're merely property; you're not imagining any real romance in Kay's latest dirty deal?

Marta   You don't know your wife very well.

Marta *lugs the last suitcase out of the house.*

Alan (*after her*)   My wife doesn't know my wife very well. That's the crux of the matter!

Alan *paces and eats a packet of cashew nuts distractedly before taking out his notebook and writing . . .*

Scene Nine

Marta *and* **Kay**'s *flat.* **Marta** *is alone unpacking a large cardboard box.*

There are a few curling photographs and unopened pink envelopes inside the box. Also a still-wrapped gift. Every item has a tell-tale yellow Post-it with her name on it.

Marta *opens a pink envelope; inside is a child's birthday card with several bank notes tucked inside. It's the same with another she opens, and another . . .*

At last she opens the pink parcel. It contains a jewellery box with a ballerina inside. **Marta** *watches the little dancer turn a few stiff pirouettes . . .*

Kay *enters* (*from work*), *her phone glued to her ear in the middle of what's clearly a heated confrontation.*

Kay   Bull . . . I have the lodgement slips right here . . .

She exchanges a distracted embrace with **Marta**, *before locating the contested payslips.*

Three thousand to your current account, another fifteen hundred to clear the credit card . . . It was the fourteenth – the day before yesterday . . . You can't live on a thousand a week? I'm not making a compliment of paying for my

children, I'm saying – What I'm saying is . . . Listen to me –
Okay, fine, but not at the house. Not at the – I don't want to
meet you at the house . . .

The intercom buzzer sounds. **Kay** *motions for* **Marta** *to get it.*

Kay   I am not 'afraid' of anything. You sound hysterical.
Why don't you borrow one of your mother's beta-blockers Al
– Yes, I do want to meet. We need to talk. 'Talk', Alan, no
hands. Can you do that?

Marta *returns with a registered letter.* **Kay** *signs for it and* **Marta**
returns the slip – the telephone call continuing throughout.

Kay   Alan – Alan, listen to me! I do not want to meet you in
the house because *I* cannot trust you, *you* cannot trust you –
and until one or both of us can trust you, I think it's better
we meet somewhere public, somewhere that will help you
not to humiliate yourself . . . Don't drag the kids into this, it's
got fuck-all to do with . . . I'm sorry – (*Restraining herself.*) –

Marta *takes the box of her father's possessions through to the*
bedroom, out of ear shot.

Kay   The library. Two fifteen. That's what I suggested in
the first – I'll need to leave at three fifteen to collect Claire
from [school] –

Kay *follows* **Marta** *through to the bedroom, the cordless phone glued*
to her ear and a whiskey secure in hand. She begins taking off her
shoes etc.

Marta *stows away the birthday cards in order, leaves out the*
jewellery box.

Kay   You don't *ask* an eleven year old if she wants to see her
mother! Of course she would say that if only to stop you
whinging and blubbering. She's taking care of you, Alan;
you're letting an eleven-year-old child feel responsible for
you! (*Groans with frustration.*) What? What are you talking
about? No one touched me. That was a sigh, Alan, an
expellation of stale air – I'm going to hang up now. I'll see

you at the library. Two fifteen. Have a bloody cold shower first!

She throws the phone on the bed, undresses during the following.

Kay Seventeen years of near celibacy and now all he wants to do is fuck me.

She begins to light a cigarette.

Marta Not in the bedroom. Please.

Kay Every time I arrange to see him he arrives with an erection which, I'm told, is my responsibility. My perversion has done this to him. According to Alan I have made myself 'an icon of fuckability'. Can you believe it?

Marta How can there be such an ugly word – 'fuckability'?

Kay It's Alan's triumph of the week. I can see him – knocking cups off the bedside locker, groping to get a pen so he can memorialise it. The strange thing is – he used to be quite squeamish about that sort of language. When we first met he used to flinch when I said 'fuck'.

Marta What about the children? You didn't talk about Claire and Myles?

Kay I tried to discuss our children. Unfortunately his erect penis doesn't appear to have ears. (*Noticing.*) Your father's things . . .

Marta You should put the phone down when he talks about anything other than the children. Don't reward him.

Beat.

Do you think Claire would want this?

Marta *indicates the jewellery box.*

Kay Yes, no – I don't know. I imagine she'd rather a sawn-off shotgun she could shoot me with . . . Fuck!

Kay *has difficulty opening her bra clasp.*

Marta Let me . . .

Marta *undoes it, massages* **Kay**'s *shoulders.*

Kay   That serious look Claire has when she looks at you across a room? Myopia. I saw the optician's bill on the Visa statement and I rang them. She might grow out of it, the optician says. I had to ask her what kind of frames she gave her – what did they look like – I could hear the confusion on the other end of the line, the suspicion – we all know what kind of mother doesn't see her own children.

Marta   You could wait for her at the school.

Kay   I did. He took her out of class ten minutes early and skipped her tennis lesson entirely. I felt like a stalker – hanging around the school gates, hoping to steal a glance at my own daughter . . .

Marta   I'm sorry . . . It will get better, I promise.

Kay   When? When I'm dead?

Beat.

She has stopped answering my calls. Instead I'm getting a barrage of text messages . . .

Kay *reads her text messages.*

Kay   'Leave Dad alone, we hate you.' 'PS Myles hates you too.' 'I never want to see you again ever.' 'You are a liar.' 'Stop telling lies about Dad.' 'No one wants to talk to you, stop calling.' Oh and my favourite – came in four installments, there might have been more if she'd topped up her credit . . . 'Bitch bitch bitch bitch bitch bitch bitch bitch . . .'

Marta *takes the phone from her.*

Marta   It's not her talking. She's just a sponge for her father's feelings. All children are. Most of us are lucky if we ever find out what was really us and what was them.

Kay   Bastard has been telling Myles I don't want to see him. This morning when I called – I was hoping Claire would answer but Alan beat her to it – I suggested I collect both of them after school, just for a few hours – I'd have them back in time for bed if necessary. 'I'm sorry, but I can't agree to you seeing Claire and not Myles. It's simply not fair. If you want to see your daughter, you'll have to see your son too.'

Marta   But you do want to see Myles, you want to see both of your children . . .

Kay   That's exactly Alan's game plan – divide and conquer. I'm on one end of the line saying I want to see my kids – he's on the other with them listening saying I don't! Conniving fucker knows exactly how to press Claire's buttons. If she thinks 'poor Myles, Mum doesn't want to see him', she'll rally to her father AND her brother's defence! Imagine Myles soaking up that bastard's poison, thinking for one minute it's true – his mother doesn't want to see him . . .

Marta   Of course he doesn't believe that . . . He's just angry . . .

Kay   When I tried to call Claire afterwards on her mobile she wouldn't pick up. That's when the 'We hate Mum' texts started pouring in . . .

Beat.

How did I do it? How did I spend twenty years married to that manipulating, narcissistic ant-fucker!

Marta   Poor Myles . . .

Kay   It's better my son hates me. It'll make him strong.

Marta   That's not how it works, you've got to be the strong one, not him.

Kay   At the house, when Alan got physical, Myles tried to defend me.

Marta   What do you mean 'physical'? What did he do? He didn't . . . if that asshole put a finger on you . . . Kay?

Kay (*opening the letter she signed for*)   A nine-year-old trying to drag his father off his mother . . . It's so fucking sordid.

Marta   Get a solicitor, get that bastard into court and get your fucking children. They need you.

Kay *passes her the letter she's just read.* **Marta** *reads.*

Marta   Sole custody?!

Kay   And a maintenance order so I can pay for the privilege of not seeing my kids.

Kay *lights a cigarette now anyway.*

Marta (*beat*)   Fuck him. No judge is going to take children from their mother.

Kay (*taking back the letter; quotes*)   'We are confident the court will uphold the existing arrangements within the family.' That's him as primary carer and me as, you wait, I'll be portrayed as the honorary prick!

Marta   I thought he was a good guy – the first month, maybe two – I thought he seemed weak, yes, but basically good . . . I almost trusted him . . . I feel sick . . .

Kay   There's no such thing as 'weak' and 'good' – worst vipers I ever met were snivelling, apologetic little cowards – women and men. (*Several beats; noticing the jewellery box.*) My aunt bought me one of these when I was small. I broke off the ballerina and stuck my brother's farmyard pig on it.

Marta *winds the jewellery box, they listen a while together.*

Marta   My father must have sent it to me for my third birthday. My mother returned it. Look at the date on the stamp.

She hands **Kay** *the wrapping paper.* **Kay** *reads the yellow Post-it that flutters from the wrapper.*

Kay   'Marta. Cooker was paraffin, not gas. Hence *no pipe!*' What does that mean?

Marta *takes the yellow Post-it from* **Kay**, *who waits for elucidation.*

Several beats. **Marta**, *upset by the Post-it, balls it up and climbs off the bed.*

Kay   You okay?

Marta   I need a shower.

Kay   Want company?

Marta   No!

Beat.

Thanks . . .

Kay (*reaching out*)   I'm sorry. I've been distracted . . . When this shit is sorted, if this shit gets sorted . . . I need to find a way to turn the tables – to hit him where it hurts . . .

Marta   It's so fucked up it's almost funny . . .

Kay   What is?

Marta   That hating the other parent could become the measure of how much we love our kids . . .

Marta *enters the bathroom, closing it behind her.* **Kay** *winds the key on the jewellery box, lets the music play and the little ballerina pirouette beneath her finger before slamming the lid shut and collapsing in exhaustion against the bedhead.*

Scene Ten

A spotlight on **Kay** *giving her retrospective 'testimony' on the stand.*

Kay   The judge is a woman. Early fifties, a mother, I guess, from the scuffed shoes, the ruined breasts . . .

Alan is thrilled. It's embarrassing, I imagine, with other men, admitting that the wife got the nanny . . . I've seen how other women's husbands look at me. Beyond the slur, beyond their giddy insecurity, it's there – a seam of pure admiration.

The judge draws her gown across her breasts and narrows her eyes at me as Alan recounts my crimes. I can hear how the writer in him corralled his words for the occasion. How he ransacked his thesaurus for multiple ways of calling me a drunken pervert. It's all laughably predictable. Like a high-brow version of the Jerry Springer Show except we're using two children and a jumble of legal jargon instead of fists.

I'm cold on the stand. I can see my solicitor looking worried. I'm not my own best witness. I'm looking at myself from somewhere very far away, hearing a voice trying to defend why it is I didn't make formal arrangements for access until now. Why I saw my children only three times in the month after I abandoned my family.

I am not very convincing, I have to admit. I hear the gap, the deficit. Three times in four weeks? Why did I let him prevent me? I can't speak. I'm trapped in Alan's parody of me . . . I imagine winking at the judge, slapping my thigh – telling her I had a very bad case of bed head that first month, that my hair was dreadlocked from the sheets and that for the first time since I had Claire I missed two days of work – not from flu or food poisoning but from fucking.

Lights up on **Marta** *and* **Kay**'s *bedroom,* **Marta** *badgering a depressed, defeated heap in the bed.*

Marta   Come on. Get up. Let's go out and get paint. We'll do Myles's bedroom.

Kay   What for?

Marta   It's fucking peach. What nine-year-old boy wants to sleep in a peach coloured bedroom?

Kay   Painting his bedroom isn't going to hide the fact my son never sleeps here.

Marta   Fine. You lie there feeling sorry for yourself while your kids are getting brainwashed by that asshole . . . You've got to fight!

Kay   How can I?

Marta   You want to pay three thousand a month to take your children to McDonald's once a week? Don't pay. Sell the house. Put him and his fucking novel on the street.

Kay   Everything I aim at Alan I aim at them.

Marta   This is war, Kay, you don't stop to count casualties while the bullets are still flying. You think it's better they lose their mother? You don't think that will hurt them even more?

Kay   Claire and Myles love him. They love their father . . .

Marta   They love you. They won't thank you for not fighting.

No answer from the bed.

If this was a property deal you wouldn't give in. You'd put on your gloves and fight until you were the last one left standing.

Marta *leaves.*

Kay   I can't fight . . . How can I fight this war – dirty, the way I'd like – when what I'm fighting for is what he's fighting with . . .

Scene Eleven

Kay *and* **Alan**'s *home. Sound of* **Marta**'s *jewellery box throughout.*

Kay *opens the door of the darkened house and quietly mounts the stairs. She enters her daughter's bedroom, stands watching her bed a long while, before taking off her shoes and climbing in to curl around her sleeping body.*

Scene Twelve

Marta *and* **Kay**'s *flat.* **Marta** *is dividing her things between a suitcase and the bin.*

When the jewellery box finishes playing she stows it in the case along with her laptop, cables etc. The case won't close. She hesitates a moment before removing the jewellery box, then zipping the case.

Kay *enters. She's apprehensive at first but when she sees* **Marta** *packing she gets cocky. She helps herself to a generous pour of whiskey, drinks quietly for a few moments waiting for the storm to break.*

Kay   Aren't you going to ask me where I've been? Why I didn't call?

Marta   You want to fuck your husband, that's your business. I don't do the jealous wife routine.

Kay   Poor Alan. I think he was disappointed. As if I should have learnt a few new tricks. Maybe he imagined he'd lost something much better than he'd ever had.

Kay *kicks off her shoes, flops down on the couch.*

We did it on the couch – our inaugural couch, where you left an imprint of the leather buttons on my back . . . Three minutes. That's how long it takes him to detonate. I watched the clock. Not out of boredom, I just needed a face to look at that wasn't his.

Several beats.

Aren't you going to gnash your teeth and ask me why?

Marta   Why you're here?

Kay   I made a list this morning while Alan was in the shower. 'Ten reasons to fuck your ex-husband.' One . . .

Marta   Is this really necessary?

Kay   Not 'necessary', no, but possibly enlightening. The next time you seduce la madre de familia you'll be familiar with the architecture of betrayal. Number one. It's not entirely uncommon for wives to have non-procreative sex with their husbands, especially when . . . Two, he's entitled. Or at least that's what he's been clamouring for – a fuck for the road, the goodbye shag, standard fare, it seems, in these proceedings. Three, it was all either of us could offer that wasn't a fight. Four, I thought I might be able to control Alan more effectively with my legs wrapped around his back.

Five, because I was stupid for thinking number four, and six
. . . What was number six? Oh yes, how could I forget – for
purposes of comparison – your fingers versus 'the real
thing'. The latter might well have won out there if it hadn't
been for its most unfortunate attachment to Alan. Seven, I
thought it would be wise to relieve him of the compelling
distraction of his erection if, eight, I wanted to raise the
spectre of a civil post-coital conversation because nine . . .
(*Almost breaking.*) Nine, I didn't want to meet my children in
a park or bowling alley or a happy-meal McDonald's with
the other once-a-week wreckages. I wanted to be there,
under the same roof where my children were sleeping . . .

Kay *faulters.* **Marta** *softens, approaches.* **Kay** *rallies, moves away.*

Kay   Don't you want to hear number ten? I fucked Alan to
punish you. I want you to suffer for what you've cost me, I
want you to fucking pay. All night long I lay awake under the
weight of his leg so you wouldn't be able to sit here in front
of your fucking text-book mothers and their text-book
children passing judgement on me!

Kay *clears the mantel with one swipe, sending all the framed
pictures, family memorabilia etc crashing to the floor.*

Kay *howls with rage and grief.*

Marta *brings* **Kay** *a pair of shoes, places them beside her bare feet.*

Marta   Go home.

Marta *prepares to leave.*

Kay   I didn't fuck him. He insisted on reading to me from
his book – can you imagine? He wanted my advice on the
'wife's perspective'.

She laughs bitterly.

Marta   I wanted to make family with you, not destroy it . . .
Go back.

Marta *leaves.*

Kay   There's no going back. How can I go back – to what?

Scene Thirteen

Alan and Kay's house. Kay is patiently trickling coffee into Alan's laptop with one hand, while sipping coffee with another. Alan enters, dumps his keys, removes his jacket. He's thrown to find her at home before him.

Alan   Ah. I didn't notice the broomstick parked outside. Came back for the silver, did you?

Kay   How was your mother's funeral?

Alan   Quite jolly as a matter of fact. I told the relatives you were recovering from black stilt influenza, a kind of same-sex mutation of swine flu . . .

She sips her coffee, props it on his desk where she's standing.

Kay   I've been admiring your 'constellation' of wedding speeches. This one's my favourite. Planet B, Bob and Ann . . . It's very amusing.

Alan   They've been postponing the wedding for ten years. Until she got down to a size fourteen, apparently. These are the kind of 'personal details' the best man thought I might be able to use in his speech. You made coffee . . .

Kay   Yes, several jugs . . . Poor Bob. Ten years it takes for her to say 'yes', now he has no hair to celebrate his wedding. What was she waiting for – better or worse?

Alan   The best man's speech is supposed to cover the cracks, not illuminate them.

She stretches out leisurely on the leather couch.

Kay   Marta loved fucking on this couch – said the smell of leather reminded her of her father . . . She never knew him. He beat Marta's mother so she exorcised him from her daughter's life.

Alan   That's what turned the screw, is it! That's what set her on her mission of wife-pinching and home-wrecking?

Marta   She went to see him after her mother died. To stage, I imagine, the long-overdue reckoning. She had an elaborate outline of how it would go – what she'd say, how she'd say it . . . First she'd enumerate her father's crimes, then move on to their consequences. Next would be his admission of guilt. That was to be his punishment, you see, recognition of his crimes. The plan was that she would hold the mirror up to her father and when he recognised his own reflection he'd –

Alan   What? Shrivel like a vampire before a crucifix?

Several beats.

Kay   I have a proposition, I want to make a deal with you.

Alan   In order to 'make a deal' there must be a mutuality of leverage. What do you imagine you have that I could possibly still want?

Kay   'A mutuality of leverage.' You wrote that in your novel . . .

Alan   I wrote that in my *revised* novel. (*Suspicious.*) Which you haven't seen. Which no one has seen . . .

Moves to his desk and tries to boot his computer. **Kay** *refills her coffee.*

Alan   What did you do?

Kay   Coffee tastes shit – like you recycle the same bitter grinds over and over again . . .

Alan   What have you done?

Kay   Microsoft were very concerned. They asked me if I was sure I wanted to permanently delete all items and I confirmed, yes, I authorise a permanent delete.

Alan   You didn't . . .

He rummages frantically, finds the jagged shards of countless CDs etc.

Kay Every disc, every back up – smashed or erased. I wiped your slate clean. Except for two copies, that is. The first an early draft I've emailed to Marta, I thought she might find the date interesting. Do you realise you had me fucking her before I ever did?

Alan It was a fiction! Not a fucking prescription for you to strap on a dick and fuck your entire family in the ass!

Kay The latest version is dated just this morning, I noticed . . . I emailed that to myself before deleting. The dedication was very touching. 'For my mother . . .' Strange how relations with our parents gain such posthumous grace.

Alan You cunt.

Kay Don't worry. I saved the seven deadly wedding speeches. (*Hands him a disc.*) Marta and I lay in bed one morning and imagined the speech you would write if we were to have a wedding – we almost logged onto your website and gave you our anonymous details. I said we would have to invent too much but Marta disagreed, she said the more transparent we were the less you would recognise us.

Alan Give me back my book.

Kay You're not really in a position to make demands right now. I'd try negotiating if I were you.

Alan What makes you think I wouldn't pick up that poker right now and beat you within an inch of your life?

Kay Because I'm nearer to the poker than you are. Besides, you love your novel more than you hate me.

Several beats.

Alan What do you want?

Kay Don't make our children pay for their parents' fuck-ups.

Alan What's the goddamn 'deal'?

Kay   I'll give you back your beloved novel when you give me back my children.

Kay *lays her key down on the table.*

Kay   My key. Don't worry. I haven't kept a copy . . .

Kay *leaves. At last when he hears the Jeep depart,* **Alan** *moves to the bureau, finds a letter from a clipped pile and dials the number on it.*

Alan   Alan Freedman speaking, could you put me through to the editor's office, please . . . (*Listens.*) Yes, he should do. It's in connection with a manuscript I sent him – a novel . . . (*Listens.*) Unsolicited, yes. I did email an enquiry beforehand and he agreed to read [it] – Freedman – F-R-E-E-D-M-A-N. The novel was called 'Fucking Nanny'. I sent it almost two months ago. A hard copy by registered delivery, your agency confirmed receipt of it on the sixth . . . (*Waits.*) Yes, I know that he 'felt it wasn't for him', I have the rejection letter in hand. I'm just wondering if he might have the manuscript still – if it's perhaps on file . . . (*Listens.*) No, I didn't send a stamped S.A.E. for its return because it's bloody cheaper to print another copy! (*Listens.*) Sorry, I beg your pardon. I'm in a bit of a heap here, my house has been burgled, you see, and my computer with all my files on it destroyed, I was hoping I might be able to rescue a copy of the manuscript – (*Listens.*) You're quite certain? There's no possibility it escaped the shredder? I got the impression Mr Davies thought it showed some promise, I've reworked it since, given it a thorough overhaul in light of his comments – if I could just speak to him briefly, perhaps it's sitting forgotten on a bedside locker or overlooked on the back of a shelf, he might remember something – (*Listens several beats; at last.*) Yes, of course, I understand. Mr Davies must have a great deal of unwanted jetsam washed up on his desk. I'm sorry for bothering you. Thank you for your time.

He replaces the phone, sits for a long time in silence, contemplating the situation. The phone rings but he doesn't bother to answer it. It goes through to the answering machine. We hear a timid man's voice.

Best Man   Hi Alan, it's me, Bob and Anna's best man. Just letting you know I won't be needing the speech after all. Wedding's off. Sorry 'bout that, mate. Not sure if I still need to post the final draft payment or not. Anyway, let me know, you have my number, cheers.

Alan *cracks the disc containing the wedding speeches in half. Lights.*

Scene Fourteen

Kay *and* **Alan***'s home, six years later.*

The house is emptied of all but a few remaining boxes and containers. A huge 'FOR SALE – PRICE REDUCED' sign hangs outside. The light is gloomy, it's late afternoon on a winter's day.

Claire*, now 17, vacuums around the packed boxes. A short struggle against the swollen front door and* **Kay** *enters. She watches* **Claire** *for several spellbound moments, unseen by her daughter.*

Claire *switches off the vacuum, moves boxes so she can vacuum underneath.*

Kay *tries the light switch.*

Claire   It's no use. Bulb's gone. Dad was too mean to buy a new –

She quietens on seeing who it is. Several beats.

Kay   I was passing, the door was open – just about . . .

Beat.

Happy belated birthday . . .

Claire *makes a point of ignoring her.*

Kay   I hear you're following in your father's footsteps, hoping to do medicine.

Claire   Who told you that? Myles?

Kay   No, your brother didn't betray you. I read it on your Facebook.

Claire *pointedly continues packing/stacking a few boxes.*

Kay   Look at you . . . It's like seeing myself through frosted glass – or under water . . .

Claire   You look old.

Kay *examines two height measurement marks on the wall.*

Kay   'Claire, eleven . . . Myles, nine . . .' Marta did that, do you remember?

Claire   Dad will be back from the clinic soon. His shift finishes at six.

Claire *cleans the measurement marks off the wall.*

Kay   You got the iPod I sent . . . I wasn't sure if you would. Or if Alan's still dashing to the letterbox to confiscate my letters . . .

Claire   I decide who deserves to be in my life. Dad's got nothing to do with it.

Kay   That's very loyal of you, Claire – and very naïve.

Claire   Fuck you. You don't know who I am. Dad doesn't have to tell me what a cow you are, I remember.

Kay   What? What do you actually remember, Claire? And what have you been told?

Claire *switches on the vacuum again.* **Kay** *plugs it out so the flex of the vacuum stretches the distance between them like an umbilical chord.*

Kay   Claire –

Claire   You ran off and left us – not Dad, you. So don't come here trying to make out Dad's the bad guy. Even before you left you were no good; Dad was the one who took care of us, you were too busy doing your dirty deals and screwing our nanny!

Kay   I left my marriage, not my children. And in some bizarre way, Alan was party to that too . . . Even me not loving – (*Several beats.*) I don't mean that, I mean me being afraid to love you . . .

Claire   You admit it.

Kay   Yes, I admit it, I was scared . . . When that tiny premature creature peered out at me from its glass tank – I thought my heart would stop with panic. You were so fragile, darling . . . so breakable . . . I used to have nightmares that I was carrying you in my arms and you tumbled out . . . Or that I put you in my pocket but there was a hole in it and when I reached in to get you, you were gone . . . You were so relaxed in your father's hands, in mine you squirmed like a fish –

Claire   Yeah, well, maybe I knew something I shouldn't . . . Do you mind? I have stuff to do . . .

She switches on the vaccuum again. **Kay** *plugs it out so the flex of the vaccuum stretches the distance between them like an umbilical chord.*

Kay   Please. Hear me out, Claire. I'm not asking for anything more than that.

Claire *steps on the retract button so the electric chord recoils noisily into the vaccuum.*

Claire   So, you had fantasies of killing me. What else? Make it quick. One of us here has a life . . .

Kay   I watched Alan with you and it was different. He had no fear; for the first time since I'd known him your father oozed confidence. When he held you in his arms he glowed with that same triumphant instinct he accused me of having only when I was buying or selling something . . . The nurses set up a camp bed for him between your cot and me. He bought a pump, expressed milk from my breasts and fed you while I slept . . .

You were almost two weeks old when I tried to feed you for the first time. I remember – I'd woken before Alan and I was lying in bed looking through the bars of your cot watching you sleep . . . There was a little spit here on your lips and every time you exhaled you blew a tiny bubble . . . The bubble would burst when you inhaled but then when you breathed out again the bubble would reappear . . . (*Several beats.*) I carried you to the conservatory to the farthest end of the house. When you woke I opened my nightshirt and tried to put my nipple in your mouth . . .

Claire   Oh, sick.

Claire *puts on her headphones.*

Kay   You wouldn't drink. Your whole body stiffened, you started screaming . . . Alan came then. Even though we were so far away with all the doors between us closed he must have heard you . . . He came dashing in, tripping over his pyjamas legs, and grabbed you out of my arms. The way he looked at me, the way he glared at my open shirt . . .

Claire (*headphones on*)   I'm not listening. I can't hear a word you're saying . . .

She ups the volume on her iPod; **Kay** *pulls the headphones from her.*

Claire   Stay away from me!

Kay   Fine. I'll stay away. But you're going to hear this Claire – not for me, for you. Because one day, if you're lucky, you're going to be a mother and you're not going to like yourself very much if you keep hating me!

Claire *has won the headphones back but doesn't put them on – yet.*

Claire   Finish what you have to say and get out.

Kay   Alan heated a pack of expressed milk from the freezer and fed you. Over the next week, he weaned you onto formula. By the time your brother was born, the deal was done. I took thirty-six hours parental leave, sixteen of them labour.

Claire   You're proud of that . . .

Kay   Yes. I was . . . Every morning at seven when I left you and Myles sleeping in your beds and reversed out of the drive I thought I was escaping something. Maybe if I had had a mother myself – or someone I could talk to . . . Your father left me nothing but a goodnight kiss and a stack of unpaid bills and I thought he was being generous. I thought he was subsidising me.

Claire   Ah, now I get it, it was Dad's fault you fucked off with Marta and left us.

Kay   I made mistakes. Your father exploited them. No doubt I exploited his. Claire –

Kay *touches* **Claire**'*s arm.*

Kay   I am sorry . . .

Claire *glares at her mother's hand on her arm.* **Alan** *steps into the doorway carrying a large flashlight which he clicks on and off – to no avail.*

Alan   Damn, forgot batteries, meant to nip out and buy them at lunch but Harrington corralled me into an hour at the [driving range] – Who let her in?

Claire (*to her father*)   She says she sent me this . . .

Claire *shows her father the iPOD.*

Alan (*bluffing*)   Don't listen to her, the woman's a pathological fantasist.

Kay   You wrote that in your book too . . . It's all there, Claire, in his own words . . .

She takes the manuscript from her bag, offers it to **Claire**. **Alan** *snatches it, sets it alight and stuffs it in the Aga.*

Alan *puts his arm around his daughter's shoulders.*

Alan (*to* **Claire**)   Come on, let's get out of here. Leave the vulture to her carcass.

Claire *shrugs off her father's arm.*

Kay   You're not leaving without a toast? The war's lost if not over, surely we can crawl out of our trenches to share a civil drink?

Kay *produces a bottle of champagne from her bag and pops the cork.*

Kay   What shall we drink to? (*No one answers.*) Come on, Alan, let's have a killer toast from the best man!

Alan   Wait in the car, Claire. I'll finish up here.

Claire *doesn't move; she watches her parents together.*

Kay   I know. How about your line from the book where you and I toast our settlement – 'Our mutual losses, our fictitious gains . . .'

Alan   'Our mutual losses, our *deadly* gains.'

The correction betrays something. **Alan** *notices his daughter looking at him strangely.*

Alan   I said, wait in the car, Claire.

Claire *exits, brushing roughly off her father's shoulder as she cuts a direct path to the door. The moment of her daughter's departure is a difficult one for* **Kay** *– especially with* **Alan** *as witness.*

Once he is sure **Claire** *is gone* **Alan** *removes a folded document from his pocket, hands it to* **Kay***.*

Kay (*the document*)   Myles's school fees . . .

Alan *proceeds to the door with a stack of boxes. Before he exits.*

Alan   His first term payment is overdue. If it's not lodged by the end of the month there's a stiff penalty to be paid.

Alan *exits.*

We hear the car engine turning as **Kay** *looks for something to drink her champagne in. In the miscellaneous debris left behind she finds a mug – an old 'Best Dad in the World' mug with a broken handle . . .*

In the reversing arc of **Alan***'s headlights we see* **Kay** *fill the mug with champagne and toast the empty house.*

Kay   'Best Dad in the world . . .'

She slugs back her champagne, hurls the cup against the chimney breast, leaves.

Several beats on the empty stage.

Snuff to black.